Acknowledge; Beware and Recognize

By

Audrey F. Evans-Ford

This book is a work of fiction. Places, events, and situations in this story are purely fictional. Any resemblance to actual persons, living or dead, is coincidental.

© 2002 by Audrey F. Evans-Ford. All rights reserved.

No part of this book may be reproduced, stored in a retrieval system, or transmitted by any means, electronic, mechanical, photocopying, recording, or otherwise, without written permission from the author.

ISBN: 1-4033-9491-1 (e-book)
ISBN: 1-4033-9492-X (Paperback)

This book is printed on acid free paper.

CONTENTS

Acknowledgements vii
My Very Special Thanks ix
"And A Very, Very, Very Special Thank You" To: xi
Weapons xiii
My Dedication xv
Your Seed, Your Tree xvii
Why Did I Write This Book? xviii
Acknowledge Satan xx
Beware and Recognize xxv

"ACKNOWLEDGE SATAN IS AT WORK" 1
   Satan's Weapons 1
   PSALM 121 4
   The Dream Attacker 5
   Satan Loves to Say "I Told You" 8
   "Life" 11
   Psalm 145 (Edited) 12
   Living to Impress 13
   From Psalm 37 15
   "GREED" 16
   Money, What About It? 17
   What is Halloween? 20
   Cleanliness and Clearness 22
   We Can Stop This "Madness" 24
   We Must Save Our Children 27
   A Book for All Children 30

"BEWARE AND KNOW" 32
   Contradictive 32
   Selfishness 35
   My Addiction 37
   Words of Comfort and Strength Psalm 34 40
   Tough Love 41
   "TOUGH LOVE OR MERCY?" 43
   "The Choice is Yours!" 43
   The Agony 45
   Why Do I Cry? 48
   The Joy of Suffering 49

"AGONY"	52
The Times I forgot About Jesus	53
I Will Remember	55
The Principle of Life	56
RECOGNIZE SATAN'S WORK"	**58**
Obedient to The Right Voice	58
Obeying The Ministry	62
"STRESS"	64
Then and Now	65
Religion is Division	68
Eve and Adam	71
The Commandment of Marriage	74
The Walk	80
PSALM 124	83
The Comforter	84
Why Have Faith In God?	87
"DOUBT"	90
When Am "I" Important?	91
The Pop Quiz	92
"Love Thy Enemy!"	94
"GOD NEVER LEFT AND GOD NEVER LEAVES!"	**99**
I Said I Can't!	99
Don't! Give up	101
Words of Encouragement from Psalm 37	104
Praying	105
"SHAME"	107
"Soul" What is it?	108
Before I Exist No More	111
Be Determined!	112
You Are Never Alone!	116
JEREMIAH CHAPTER 45	120
Application of Strength	121
Psalm 27 (Revised)	124
DO YOU WANT A BETTER LIFE?	**125**
Do You Really Know God?	125
Psalm 85	130
The Decision!	131
Psalm 86	133
I Am Not Really A Sinner!	134

Have You Made Your Decision? 137
Psalm 21 Revised 141
"Joy in the Salvation of the Lord" 141
Two Years of Stumbling 142
"IF" 144
A Plan 145
The Bible 147
Sit or Stand! 150
The Summary 154
"DRUGS" 157
AFFORD 158
About the Author 159

Acknowledgements

Thank you Shirley McMillian for your friendship and sharing. Thank you for sharing your book by Max Lucado with me, "No Wonder They Call Him The Savior" This book really enlightened me and helped me in my struggle surrendering my life to Jesus Christ.

Even though I have never meet Max Lucado and Iyanla Vanzant, I want to acknowledge and thank them for their books, "No Wonder They Call Him The Savior" by Lucado and "One Day My Soul Just Opened Up! by Vanzant.

Thank you Inspiration Cable Television for the ministries with: Dr. Joyce Meyers, Kenneth and Gloria Copeland, Creflo Dollar, Bishop Courtney McBath, Robb Thompson, John Hagee, Maury Davis, Brad Spencer, Dr. Gerald Mann, Dr. Charles Stanley, Bishop Frank E. Ray, and Andrew Wommack, Pastor Frederick C. Price, Bishop Paul S. Morton, Bishop Jack Wallace, Pastor Pat Francis, Bishop T.D. Jake, Pastor Randy Morrison, Pastor Claude R. Alexander Jr., Pastor William Crews, Pastor Ed Young, Morris Cerullo, Rod Parsley, Pastor Gregory Powe, Pastor Gregory Dickow, Pastor Richard Lee, Pastor "Bam" Crawford, Pastor Mac Hammond and Pastor Bernard Chaney. Thank you all for helping me to believe in the unseen power of God. Thank you for being witnesses and testifying to Gods unchanging love, His mercy and His grace.

I thank God for each one of you. I thank God for restoring my soul and giving me this new life. Thank You Jesus!

My Very Special Thanks

First I thank Our Heavenly Father and Jesus Christ for giving me this new life. God is the reason that I live and have written this book. God kept His promise and saved me! Thank you Father! Thank you Jesus!

Thank you David Ford. If it had not been for our troubled unrecorded marriage and my love for you, I might not have found Jesus. I thank God for letting you be an integral part of my life that brought me closer to Him. I will always love you!

I thank God for my Daddy, Joseph B. Evans Sr. Even though my dad is deceased I will always acknowledge him. He was the one with a great big ole heart and a whole hemp, a bunch, a lots of, all the time and then some, and a hemp, a bunch more love!

Thank you Mom for your encouragement and being there for me. I thank God that He has drawn us closer through His love for the both of us! I love you Mom!

Thank you to my one and only sister Chris and to my brothers Joe and Kyle. Thank you for your unconditional love and support. Thank you for being there when I was about to give up!

Thank you Troy, Stefany and Evan. I love you so much. And of all that I have put you through and I know I put you through a lot and many times you had gotten angry with me and even hated me for a moment or two, but in your hearts you never stopped loving me nor turned your backs! Thank you God for my Children! Thank you Troy, Step and Evan! I love you guys so much!

Thank you to my wonderful nieces Trinessa and Ashley, and to my nephews Kyle Jr. (Peanut) and Marion DeAngelo!

And Thank you to my wonderful sister-in-law, Yeah, you Glo-Jean (ha,ha,ha,) I love you Gloria. Gloria there are no words that I can find to tell you how much it means to me to have your love and support. Gloria thank you and May God continue to be as good to you as He is to me! Hallelujah! Glory Be To God!

Is eight really enough? Well, I thank God for all eight of my grandchildren, Alex (Scoop), Synteria (Spring), Asia, E'lexuse (AJ), Amber (Pebbles), Trayvon (Tray), Brianna (Precious-Bre-bre) and to you too, Infinity (finny-fin) I love you all.

Even though I blew my second chance to be a good Mother, I still thank you Father God for my sweet stepchildren Andre'a, Maurice and Malcolm Ford. I love them very much and pray Father God that you will continue to watch over them and protect them!

Thank you Candice 'Carter', you are such a blessing! I love you!

Now Ruthie! Did you really think that I would forget to thank God for my Best Friend, Ruthie L. Alberry? If anyone asked me to spell friend, I would spell it R U T H I E! I love you!

Thank You Father God for "Aunt Millie" Mrs. Mary Danzler! Thank you Aunt Millie for your love, support and your many prayers!

Father God, I give to you and Christ Jesus all the honor and praise for all these wonderful people that you have filled my life with! Thank you Father, Thank you Jesus!

"And A Very, Very, Very Special Thank You" To:
You, TC,

Thank you TC for your words of TRUTH! You said to me and many other people, "You better try loving God, because Man will let you down!"

TC this was very well said, as it is very much the Truth!

There are many people that say you are crazy and you don't know what you are talking about. I know first hand, they are wrong!

I Thank You Terry for the words of knowledge and wisdom that you spoke into my life, which has given to me the desire to be closer to God and to serve Him!

Thank you TC for the "Blesssing" that you passed on to me and may God Bless You and keep you!

Thank you TC!

WEAPONS

ANGER	HATE SHAME	JEALOUSY
LUST	STRIFE	BITTERNESS
HOSTILITY	STEALING	DEPRESSION
ANXIETY	DRUNKNESS	PROFANITY
GREED	ANGER	ARROGANCE

OPPRESSION!

HOPELESSNESS

DOUBT	LIES	DRUGS	
ENVY	FIGHTING		
KILLING	FEAR	ALCOHOL	GUILT
ARGUING	DECIET	STRESS	

My Dedication

This book is dedicated to all whom have given up hope and believe that there is no hope because of their troubled lives, especially drug and alcohol users and abusers. And for those of you who believe and think that the only way out of this darkness is in death! Guess What? God loves you too! I am a living witness that God loves all His children! I too was a drug user and abuser.

Addict = Attack! You are not an addict! Satan wants you to think that you are. The drugs are his tools to destroy you and your mind. Drugs are mind-altering chemicals that Satan uses to control you. He does not want you to know God and how much God loves you. He uses the drugs to convince you that you are doomed, and there is no hope! Satan is liar! There is HOPE FOR YOU!

Are you reading this? Okay, then know that God loves you. You see, Satan had once attacked my mind and body through drugs. All glory and honor to God, I am not an addict and I never was! It was Satan all along trying to destroy me and convince me that I was a nobody, unimportant and doomed for hell. He wanted my soul and to steal me from My Father who is your Father too!

This book is dedicated to everyone that feels that he or she is caught in the snare of the devil and can't get out. This book is proof that no matter what the situation or circumstance may be God is in control. I have been redeemed, revived, recreated and filled with God's Spirit. My Father God has given me new life and has kept me in existence for the sake of showing me and you His power in order to have His name declared in all the world." And this is written in Exodus 9:16.

Gods grace and mercy is forever and for everyone! But you must surrender your life to Him! God wants you to come to Him. He wants to help and heal you. God wants you to know His power and He is waiting for you.

Look it is written that **_whoever_** calls on the name of the Lord shall be saved!" Acts 2:21. So call Him now! Confess your sins and surrender to God and be set free from the bondage of sin and worry! Look, pull a "NIKI!" and just do it. Call God! Fall on your knees and pray. If you need help in finding the right words, then hopefully these words will help you. Pray this:

Father God I know that I have been living in sin and sinned against you. I am truly sorry. In the name of Jesus please forgive me. I humble myself under your almighty hand and pray that you will quickly rescue me. I need you Father, please do not hide your face from me nor cover your ear to hear me. I am in turmoil and yes, I am afraid. Father in the name of Jesus have mercy on me! In the name of Jesus, help me Father God!

After you have prayed this prayer be assured that everything is all right and you are okay! God is with you and effectually at work helping you. Praise Him and Thank Him for His faithfulness!

Be strong and trust God. Ignore Satan and "Don't Give in to his Lies" Remember Satan is a liar! If you have truly surrendered your life to God, than know that God keeps His word. God's word has never ever returned void and it never will. He will fix what is broken, restore what is destroyed and give new life and salvation to those who call Him! Lift your hands and give to Him Praise. Watch your blessings come forth! In Jesus Name so be it!

Your Seed, Your Tree

Lord Jesus, it is your seed within me that has made me your tree.
It is your seed that grows more and more I bear good fruit!
Oh Lord, I know that I am the righteous of our Father through you. This is why I ask you Lord God, please help me to pay attention to my every thought and deed. Help me Lord to think according to your will!
Lord Jesus, I thank you that my mind has been renewed by the power of your Holy Spirit. I ask of thee, please forgive me Lord for those moments of weakness, when I allow worry to slip in. It is not my intention, nor my desire to offend you. It is usually the guilt and shame of my sin and the fear of your judgment that causes me worry.
Thank you Lord Jesus for your love that never fails and your promises that are always kept. It is your promises that bring me back to you and cancels out all my fear and worries!
Lord Jesus, You know my every thought. You know my heart. Jesus I Love you, believe in you and trust you! I worship, adore and PRAISE you, my Lord, my God!

Yes, Lord I am Yours. I am Your Seed. Your Tree!

AFFORD

Why Did I Write This Book?

Writing this book was Jesus way of restoring my soul and giving me new life. Praise God! Writing this book was my time in the wilderness that God used to prepare me spiritually, physically, mentally and emotionally to do His will. During my time in the wilderness, I have been given wisdom and knowledge to do what God has appointed me to do. I have learned to trust God, to be still in His presence and wait upon Him to act! And not to waiver no matter what the situation or circumstance that might come.

Yes, there are situations and circumstances in all of our lives that are hurting and painful and at times we feel like there is no hope at all. We are told to be patient and wait on the Lord. Guess what? That is much easier said than done. I can truly vouch for that. I have realized that the thing that causes us to be impatient is fear and anxiety. You see, we worry and become nervous and even anxious about what the outcome of our situation will be. This is a normal response to threatening situations, such as losing our spouse, family, home, finances, etc…these situations bring stress, depression and worry.

Look, deep inside we know that the cause of the problems in our lives is because we have been disobedient to the word of God? We have not been living according to God's laws. And now we fear Gods judgment! The fear causes us to be anxious and impatient with God! We want to know the outcome now! This is a no, no!

Satan will constantly remind us of our problems, suffering and pain. And while you are waiting for God to act, Satan will have you saying crazy things such as I said, "Why me, why was I even born?" Yeah, I went there. Guess what? Jesus told me, don't even try to play Him like that! Jesus, as always, was right. I was feeling sorry for myself and wanting pity. I knew why I was having so many problems in my life. I was not living according to the laws and principles of God. My problems were the result of me being disobedient to God. Satan knew this and he used my shame and guilt to hold on to me! And he will do it to you too!

Now the thing is this, I called Jesus and surrendered my life to Him. I struggled with being patient for a while, but I did it! I became still in the presence of the Lord. I stopped struggling and waited for God to act. This book is the result of me being obedient and patiently waiting on God!

"NEWSFLASH" Satan has no love for you nor I. And it brings him so much joy taking our joy! Satan cheers every time we shed a tear! Let me tell you something, every time Satan causes us to be impatient, he causes us to lose out on God's best for us and His blessings. Satan gets a big kick out of deceiving us! But it "Ain't no thang!" God our Father tells us to have no fear, because "He Is Always HERE!"

I have written this book because it was the will of God, and it is the will of God that it has been published. It is the will of God that this book is in your possession! I hope and pray that after you have read this book in its entirety that you will give Jesus a chance in your life. I did! You are reading what Jesus has done for me!

Thank you Jesus!

Acknowledge Satan

As, a Christian, (one who believes in Jesus Christ) I think that I can say that the statement I am about to make validates some truth. "I believe that many Christians would much rather stay focused on Jesus Christ, than to have any thought whatsoever about Satan." I can understand this. As a Christian I too, would rather not think about Satan either! But, I have to and so do you! We do not want to think about Satan because we know his mission is to destroy us!

We have heard of and we know about the evils of Satan, therefore many of us are afraid to think or to even speak his name. Well, here is a "Special Bulletin" report! Rather we like it or not, we have to acknowledge Satan. The reason that we must acknowledge him is because Jesus tells us in 1 Peter 5:8 that we must "Be Careful" and watch out for Satan because he is our greatest enemy!"

Here is some very good news for you. There is no need for anyone to fear Satan! Why? Just like you and I, he is Gods creation. Here is another reason; God did not create anything that is bad or evil. In fact in the Holy Bible in the Book of Genesis it is written that God saw all of His creations to be very "GOOD!"

Satan was not always a Devil. Satan was Our Fathers favorite angel! Yes, that is what I said. Satan was Gods most precious, beautiful and perfect angel. He was flawless and faultless from the day of his creation, until unrighteousness was found in him. (Ezekiel 28:15). His name was Lucifer. And God loved him!

But, Lucifer became jealous of God and wanted to be God! Lucifer was not satisfied any longer just being God's favorite angel, he wanted to be above our Father God! He wanted the praise! Lucifer said to the heavens that he would go up, up above the stars of God and he would lift up Gods throne. Lucifer said that he would make himself resemble the Most High, God. (Isaiah 14:12-14) Lucifer waged war in heaven. Heaven being heaven, with nothing but the perfect love and peace of God, Lucifer was cast out. He is no longer an angel. He is the beast, the serpent! When Satan was thrown down to earth, he came down in great anger and knowing he has very little time here, Satan has declared war on all of Gods children! That means you as well as me!

Satan war on earth began with Gods creation of the first man, "Adam". Satan attacked Adam through the help made for him, the first woman "Eve". It is written in Genesis 3:1-4 that, "the serpent proved to be the most cautious of all the wild beasts of the field that God had made. And Satan began to say to the Eve; "is it really so that God said you must not eat from every tree of the garden?" And at this Eve said to the serpent (Satan): "Of the fruit of the trees of the garden we may eat. But, as for eating of the fruit of the tree that is in the middle of the garden, God said, "We must not eat from it, nor touch it that we will not die." "At this the serpent (Satan) said to the woman (Eve): "You positively will not die!" Satan's war on earth with man begins. Eve did not know that Satan was evil. Satan lied and Eve died!

I believe that out of all of Gods creations, Satan is the busiest of all! He does not get tired and he does not quit! Satan has been and he is still busy trying to take our souls. And check this out! There is no age discrimination! He steals children too! In Hebrews 2:14 it is written, "Therefore, since the "young children" are sharers of blood and flesh, he also similarly partook of the same things, that through His (Jesus) death He might bring to nothing the one having the means to cause death, that is, the Devil."

Satan is bold! He does not care who your mother or father is. Hey, Satan even tried to tempt the Son of God, our Lord and Savior Jesus Christ. **Remember, I said he "TRIED" to tempt Jesus!**

It is written in the book of Matthew 4:5-10 that Jesus had been lead by the spirit into the wilderness to be tempted by the Devil. Then, "the Devil took Jesus along into the Holy city, and he stationed Him upon the battlement of the temple and said to Jesus, "If you are the son of God, hurl yourself down; for it is written, He will give His angels a charge concerning you, and they will at no time strike our foot against a stone. Jesus said to Satan, "You must not put the Lord our God to the test!" Satan did not give up! He took Jesus along to an unusually high mountain, and showed Him all the kingdoms of the world and their glory, trying to tempt Jesus saying to Him, "All these things I will give you if you fall down and do an act of worship to me!" Jesus told Satan to go away! "For it is written, it is God my Father whom you must worship and it is to Him alone you must render service!" Then the Devil left him!

Do you think Satan stopped there? Do you think that Satan has given up? Of course not, he is still busy as ever. He is attacking Gods children today, right now. Even as I write this book, he has attacked me many times! Oh and I am sure that there are more attacks to come. After all, Satan attacked Jesus with temptation every chance he thought that he could. And we know that Jesus was and still is perfect and we are not! So you know Satan is not about to give us a break. Okay!

Yes, Demons do exist and you are to be aware of them. Demons are to Satan what Angels are to God! Demons serve Satan by entering the bodies of God's children and taking control of their minds, hoping to steal their souls! It is written in Luke 8:27-36 that Jesus cast out demons. It is written that, As Jesus got out onto land a certain man from the city who had demons met Him. Jesus asked him: "What is your name?" He said: "Legion" because many demons had entered into him. It is written that, "those who had seen it reported to them how the demon possessed man had been made well."

It is also written in Luke 11:14 that, Jesus later expelled a dumb demon. And after the demon came out, the dumb man spoke and the crowd marveled. It is by the means of God finger that Jesus expelled the demons. Yes, Demons like their god Satan, they too exist. It is imperative that we acknowledge them and beware of them.

We must be aware of Satan and his demons because it is written in 1 Timothy 4:1 that, "However, the inspired utterance says definitely that in later periods of time (now) some will fall away from their faith, paying attention to misleading inspired utterances and teachings of demons." The book of Revelations, chapter 16:14 speaks of, "expressions inspired by demons and perform signs and they go forth to the kings of the entire inhabited earth, to gather them together to the war of the great day of God the Almighty." Therefore, as it is written in James 4:7 "Subject yourselves, to God; but oppose the Devil and he will flee (for awhile) from you!"

Oh, but know that he will come back. So be careful and watchful and Pray for discernment!

In the Holy Bible in 1 Peter 5:8-9 we are told to keep our senses and "Be watchful for our adversary the Devil, walks about like a roaring lion, seeking to devour you (us)." Take your stand against him and be solid in the faith, knowing that the same things in the way of your sufferings are being accomplished in the entire association of your brothers in the world. In Ephesians 6:11 we are told to "Put on the complete suit of armor from God that we maybe able to stand firm against the machinations of the Devil, Satan himself!" Do not, I repeat! Do not be afraid of Satan, there is no need to. Remember this, Satan is a creation of God, just like you and I. Our Father and our Savior has authority over all creation.

Satan existence because:

1. God created him and God loved him as he loves us. God gave to Satan the same things that he has given to us, a free will. God allowed Lucifer to make his own choice. Lucifer chose to go against God and be defiant! Lucifer became rebellious and evil.

2. God allows Satan to exist for the same reason that he allows you and I to exist, "For the sake of showing His power and in order to have His name declared in all the earth" this is written in the Book of Exodus 9:16. All Power is Gods! God has the authority over all of His creation, even when it has turned from good to evil! God's power is forever great and almighty!

It is imperative that we acknowledge that Satan does exist and that he is very busy. Satan never sleeps and he never gets tired. Satan mission is to destroy us!

There is nothing to fear. Acknowledge Satan and his demons so that you can recognize their work and be aware of them! Praise God and thank Him for giving you knowledge of Satan and thank God for His love and mercy!

"STAY ON GUARD WITH GOD!"

Beware and Recognize

Now that we have acknowledged that Satan really does exist and that he is present among us, we now have to beware of him and recognize his work. And it is not quite as easy as it may sound. Remember he is the god of this world.

The only way that we can arm and protect ourselves against Satan and his cohorts is to get into the word of God. We must accept Jesus Christ as Lord over our lives and not only believe, but know that He is the Son of God! We must obey God's laws and live according to His principles!

In order to defeat Satan we have to have a plan and form our strategy. And remember that Satan has his plan already in full effect. His plan is to destroy us! We are at war with Satan and spiritual wickedness rather we like it or not. This is just the way that it is. I have already told you that it is written in Ephesians 6:11 that we must, "Put on the complete suit of armor from God that you maybe able to stand firm against the machinations of the Devil!"

Satan is a smooth operator and we need knowledge of his weapons. We need to know how he uses them. And we definitely need to know his target, which is our mind! Our mind is our central control center. And yes, Satan is going for a direct and hopefully fatal hit!

Satan uses his weapons to distract you from God hoping to cause you to slip, stumble, fall and fail! Satan tries to make you feel like you are a 'nobody', you will never be anybody and life is not worth living. Satan will have you actually wanting to die. I know. I have been there! So, watch out and be aware! Don't let Satan control your thoughts!

Look, Jesus already defeated Satan for us when He gave His life on the cross. Jesus shed His blood to redeem us. He conquered death and destroyed Satan's evil works. And because Jesus loves us, He has given us authority over all the power of the enemy, Satan. "IF" we surrender our lives to Jesus and accept Him as Lord over our lives, we can defeat Satan! Satan has no power over God! He has no power over Jesus! And Satan has no power over you, "IF" you believe in

Jesus and be obedient to the word and live according to God's principles! God always supplies us with the ammunition that we need to defeat Satan. Gods' ammunition is so power, that it not only destroys, but it gives life!

The ammunition is the "Word" the "Word of God!" It is written in the Book of John 1:1-3 that, "In the beginning the Word was, and the Word was with God, and the Word was God! All things came into existence through God, and nothing apart from God not one thing came into existence! "Not even Satan!"

The power to defeat Satan is in the Word of God. It is written in the Book of Proverbs 18:21 that, "Death and life are in the power of the tongue and he that is living in it will eat its fruitage." The power to defeat Satan is in you! The power is in your mouth! Your Tongue! God has supplied you with the ammunition to defeat Satan! His word and your tongue!

This is a book of short stories that will help you to recognize the works of Satan and to beware of him. And know that you do not have to fear him! Remember, you have been supplied with your ammunition. You will never run out of ammunition, there is plenty in stock. The Bible is overflowing with your needs. Use it!

"ACKNOWLEDGE SATAN IS AT WORK"

Satan's Weapons

I have been instructed to tell you about the weapons of our adversary, Satan and to remind you that Jesus warned us to be watchful and careful when it comes to Satan is our greatest adversary. We must acknowledge Satan, recognize his works and beware of him and remember that his mission is to destroy us!

Satan has many weapons, these are just some of them; adultery, alcohol, anger, anxiety, arrogance, back-biting, bitterness, debt, deceit, depression, disease, discouragement, doubt, drugs, drunkenness, envy, fear, fighting, frustration, gambling, gossip, greed, guilt, hate, hostility, illness, jealousy, killing, lies, lust, money, oppression, profanity, revenge, sex, shame, stress, strife and vanity. These are just some of Satan weapons. Don't be fooled, all these things can destroy you and even kill you, as well as others. Satan uses all these weapons against you.

Let's take Satan's weapon of 'hate.' Satan knows that when we hate one another, it brings anger, bitterness hostility, jealousy and envy into our hearts. See the domino effect here. Satan places hate in your heart then all his other weapons are ignited! There is an explosion! We get angry, bitter, hostile, frustrated and want to get revenge. But, in Romans 12:19 it is written that God says, "Vengeance is His!" It is written in Ephesians 4:13, God says; "Let all malicious bitterness and anger and wrath and screaming and abusive speech 'betaken away from us all' with all badness. See how Satan has used his weapon of "HATE" to distract you from the will of God and causing you to be disobedient!

Anything that distracts you from God and causes you to be disobedient to His laws and principles is a weapon of Satan.

Satan weapons are powerless if you are obedient to God's laws and principles. God's righteous children are protected. Sure Satan is going to bother you. He is going to bother you because you belong to God. Let me elaborate just a little. It is like this, if you are not a child of God, Satan has no reason to attack you. The reason for this is simple; he has no reason to attack the ones that already belong to him. Now do you understand why he is attacking you? Yes, it is because you belong to God!

Let us be honest with ourselves. We all know when we have sinned. We know rather or not we have been living according to the laws and principles of God. No one has to tell us, we know. As my Mom use to say to me, I taught you right from wrong and you know the difference. Those of us that know Jesus, we may not be able to recite the "Ten Commandments," but we know right from wrong and we know when we have sinned!

Guess what? Satan knows when you sin too. After all it is Satan himself that suggested to you to sin. Check this out. After you have sinned, Satan attacks you with his weapon of "doubt." Oh Satan is not going to let up on you! Remember he wants your soul! He is aiming for the "Bulls Eye" the fatal attack. He is aiming for your mind. Now that you have sinned, Satan is attacking you with his weapons of anger, anxiety, bitterness, depression, frustration, guilt, hate, hopelessness, stress, and shame! Satan has pulled out his heavy artillery! You are feeling the pain of all these weapons and they are causing you to "doubt" and question God. This is exactly what Satan wants you to do, be unsure, confused and doubt God!

Satan is using the weapon of doubt to convince you that our Father will not forgive you this time. Satan wants you to give up! You already know that you have sinned. You are feeling guilty and you are a shame. And Satan is rubbing it in, making you feel worst!

Satan has you feeling so guilty and a shame that you don't even want to pray! Satan has your mind so messed up that you are afraid to pray! He has convinced you that you have committed sin one time to many and God is not going to forgive you this time!

Satan is a "Liar!" This book that you are reading is proof that Satan is a "Liar!" I still fall short every now and then. But, I can honestly tell you that I am not the sinner that I used to be! Praise God! I am have been made righteous through Jesus Christ!

Stop letting Satan mess with your head! Remind that fool (Satan) that God sent His only begotten son Jesus Christ into this world to redeem you and save you from your sins! Remind Satan that Jesus paid the price for your sins in full with His precious blood. Remind Satan of the written word in 1John 1:7,9 that, "If we walk in the light as He (God) is in the light we have fellowship with one another and the blood of Jesus Christ His Son cleanses us from all sin." And "If we confess our sins, He is faithful and just to forgive us our sins and to cleanse us from all unrighteousness!"

Remember, Jesus loves us rather we are willing to admit it or not. Jesus love for us is greater than our love is for Him. So, know that Jesus always forgives. Jesus love for us is so awesome that He will not by any means recall our sins and our lawless deeds to our mind ever! And this is written in the book of Hebrew 10:17-18. It is true Jesus keeps no record of our sins. So if Jesus does not remember our sins, then why should you? Have you asked Jesus to forgive you for your sins? If you have, then forget about them! Jesus has!

Remember to acknowledge the existence of Satan. Recognize Satan's weapons and his works. Beware of them and be prepared for his attacks, at all times! Satan is determined to destroy all of us!

And don't forget, Our Father God has given to us a weapon far greater than any weapon than Satan has. We have His "WORD!" And no weapon formed against God's children shall prosper!

So Don't just stand on the word of God, "USE IT!"

Audrey F. Evans-Ford

PSALM 121

I look up to the mountain – does my help come from there?
My help comes from the Lord! Who made the heavens and the earth!
He will not let me stumble and fall; the one who watches over me will never sleep.

Indeed, He who watches over me never tires and He never sleeps.
The Lord himself watches over me! The Lord stands beside me as my protective shade.
The sun will not hurt me by day nor the moon by night.
The Lord keeps me from all evil and preserves my life.
The Lord keeps watch over me as I come and go; both now and forever!

The Dream Attacker

Oh yeah, Satan attacks you in your dreams too! I am telling you that he never, ever gives up! After a pretty good day with just a little bit of disappointing news, I fell asleep not worrying about anything. You see, I know that Jesus never sleeps and he watches over me at all times.

Well I awaken about 1:15 and 1:30 am, from an attack of Satan in my dream. He attacked me with things about my husband. And of course they were bad things. It is like this Satan knows all of our weaknesses, may it be drugs or some one that we love. Well since his attack on me with drugs has failed, he now uses my love for my husband to try and break me. He is trying to make me stumble and fall again. It is his job to do all and anything that he can to separate me from God and I can understand it. Satan is trying to get me all bent out of shape and back into sin. But, it is okay. Let me tell you why it is okay.

It is okay because Jesus loves me and protects me even when I am asleep. The disappointing news that I received that day was from my husband. Our anniversary is Saturday, November 10th. My husband and I had talked about spending it together, even though we are separated. But, when I asked my husband for confirmation about it, he said that he did not know if we would. He said he was having a bad day. Yeah, Satan was working him. Well Satan has separated us and he is dogged determined to keep us apart. I really did not think about it anymore I just prayed about it and asked Jesus to step in. I decide that rather or not David and I spend our anniversary together, that I would not stumble or fall, but that I would do whatever Jesus would have me to do!

Satan's attempt to torment me mentally failed. He was trying to upset me. It did not work. So, he attacked me in my sleep. He showed me my husband with another woman. Satan knows that there is nothing more hurting and painful than for a wife to dream, think or know about her husband being with another woman. Oh, it could be so devastating! But, the dream did not devastate me, because I knew what to do. I awaken from the dream and called Jesus. And like always, Jesus was there with me. He talked me through the attack and guess what else he did? Jesus reassured me that everything was okay and that I have nothing to worry about. He reminded me of Satan's attacks and to recognize them, even in dreams. Praise God!

Then Jesus reminded me of what He told me that He would do. Jesus reminded me that He assured me that whatever I pray for that I will have. All that I need to do is trust and believe in Him, that's all. Jesus reminded me that it is written in Isaiah 55:11 that, "His word that goes forth from His mouth will prove to be. That His word will not return to Him void! But, that His word will certainly do that in which He have delighted, and it will have certain success in that for which He have sent it!" His Word is Firm!

The Holy Spirit comforted me and my mind became filled with thoughts of Gods love and promises and things that He wants me to do. It was so awesome how my heart was filled with joy and peace. Then visions of things to come to me were presented. I begin receiving instructions to write more stories, including this one. I was shown how Satan tried to get me to prematurely finish this book. With my heart full of joy and peace and my mind filled with thoughts of Jesus, I fell off to sleep.

I told you, our greatest adversary, Satan never gets tried and never sleeps, in fact he don't even take a nap! After I had fallen off to sleep again, Satan still attacked me, this time he attacked me with a dream about a cousin of mine and I getting hi smoking crack cocaine. Now, check this out, my cousin lives real far in distant miles from where I live. Okay! How are we going to get hi together, through the telephone! Satan uses such stupid things to try to make you fail. Unfortunately, some of us do fall and fail. Satan is trying to convince me that Jesus will not answer my prayers. Duh! Wrong! Satan is a Liar! Oh, and by the way, Jesus never sleeps either!

I know at this present time that my husband is caught in the snare of the Devil. It is the work of Satan that is keeping us separated and he is determined to keep us apart. I am here to tell you that Satan is a liar. So David and I will not spend our anniversary together. Is my marriage dead? No problem. Jesus resurrected and still resurrects the dead. Is it going to take a miracle? Jesus performs miracle too! Jesus Keeps His Promises, His Word Will Not Return Void!

Acknowledge, Beware and Recognize

    I know this because Jesus gave me a new life. Jesus answered my prayers as a sinner and I know that He will answer my prayers as a righteous woman. In fact I am confident that He will, because it is written in the book of Mark 11:22 that Jesus said, that I can ask anything of Him and receive it, if I believe and have no doubt in my heart! Then I have it! You see, I know that the Word of God is unchangeable and He takes delight in giving to us the desire of our heart! God's word will not return to Him void, it will prove to be! Jesus said to ask anything of Him and He will do it! I asked! And I believe in my heart that it is done!

    Yeah, Satan is a Dream Attacker and he will attack you in your dreams. Don't be afraid to go to sleep, Jesus protects us in our sleep too. Go ahead and fall asleep. Jesus never leaves us, not even when we fall asleep. So, go on, fall asleep, Jesus is watching over you!

Audrey F. Evans-Ford

Satan Loves to Say "I Told You"

The previous story that you have just read about the "Dream Attacker" is true. Yeah, Satan attacked me in my dream about my husband and another woman. Well, David is involved with another woman. In fact he says that he is involved with several women and that he is out of control. He said that he is going out of town for the weekend and that we will not spend our anniversary together. So much for that!

And guess what? Satan is now telling me that he told me so! Satan is rejoicing because he knows that I have been disappointed. Was it David that disappointed me? No, it was not. It was Satan and his demonic spirits controlling him. David has no control over his own spirit at this particular time. Our separation and the reason for our separation have caused him to become weak and prey to the adversary. Some people turn to God during times of trouble and some of us don't know where to turn and end up getting caught in the snare of the Devil! I know that this is what happened to David, he got caught in Satan snare! He is off the chain. His heart has become hardened, especially towards me.

Yeah David said that he is going out of town and we will not spend our anniversary together. And now Satan is yelling in my ear, "I told you, you would not spend your anniversary with your David!" All right, already! It is okay and I am okay. I know that Jesus loves me and He will not fail me. Therefore I shall not let my heart be troubled! Jesus has never failed me and this is why I am okay. I will not stop praying for David. I will not stop praying for our marriage. I will not give up because to give up what I believe in, is to not trust Jesus! I know that Jesus is not a liar!

What I am telling you is this, just because Jesus does not answer your prayer when you want Him to, does not mean that He is not going to answer it. Sure it might take some time, days, months, years, but if you are sincere, don't give up! This is what Satan wants you to do. Sure I was disappointed that David and I did not spend our anniversary together. Again, I tell you that it is okay.

Acknowledge, Beware and Recognize

I know the work of Satan and I recognize it! I know that David is caught in Satan's snare he has no power over his own spirit. In the book of Proverbs it is written that, "Whoever has no rule over his own spirit is like a city broken down, without walls. David said that he prayed and ask Jesus to help him, but he is out of control. Praise God! There is nothing is impossible, absolutely nothing is impossible for Jesus! It is written in the book of Matthew that our Father has given Jesus "All Authority in the heavens and on the earth"

The Holy Spirit reminded me that David like myself has to make his choice. I was also reminded that Jesus did not force me to accept Him. He let me make that choice on my own. This is what Jesus does with each and every one of us He lets us make our own choice. I have inner peace because I love Jesus and it is my choice to surrender my life to Him. And I respect David's right to freely choose. And if David does not choose to accept Jesus in his life at this time and does not want our marriage any longer, then I accept it. But, I will not stop praying for David and I will not give up! I thank God everyday for His mercy and His grace!

Jesus knows David's every thought and his heart. I trust Jesus to help him. I realize what I have been asking Jesus to do. I thank the Lord for bringing it to my attention. I wanted Jesus to force David to surrender his life to Him. I wanted Jesus to make David love me and want to be married to me. I was asking Jesus to do something to David that He did not do to me. Jesus let me freely make my own choice and He will let David freely make his choice. Jesus will not and does not force any of us to love Him or accept Him.

Satan told me that Jesus would not answer my prayer and that David and I would not spend our anniversary together. It is true, David and I did not spend our anniversary together. But, Satan still lied.

Jesus did answer my prayer. Jesus told my why David and I did not spend our anniversary together and He helped me to understand what was really happening. Jesus still reminds me that His word will not return void and without results, but **"With Certain Success."** Jesus will rescue David from the clutches of Satan. I pray for it and I believe it! Yep! **"Satan Told Me So"** but, **Jesus "Told Me Why!"** Praise God!

Know this like you know your name. Know that Jesus has and always answers your prayers. Just because you do not see the manifestation of your prayers as soon as you want to see them, does not mean that your prayers have not been answered.

Don't look at the situation or the circumstances around you. Trust in the Lord. You must walk by Faith and not by sight! Have no doubt and never lose hope. Remember that Satan uses every opportunity to say to you, "I Told You So" hoping that you will give up! I telling you, DON"T DO IT! Jesus will not fail you!

The next time Satan says, "I told you so!" Just simply tell him "Yeah, I Know!" "JESUS TOLD MY WHY!"

Acknowledge, Beware and Recognize

**Life
In *Satan's world of*
Evilness, where there's no
Salvation!**

Audrey F. Evans-Ford

Psalm 145 (Edited)

Always exalt our Father God Almighty and bless His Holy name. Bless His name to time indefinite, forever! Praise His Holy name all day long!

God is great and His greatness is unsearchable. God is very much worthy of our praise all day long!

Generation after generation commends His works and tell about His mighty acts. They speak about Gods glorious splendor of dignity and the matters of His wonderful works and they make His works their concern.

They speak of Gods strength and fear inspiring things. They declare His greatness! They bubble over with joy mentioning His goodness and His righteousness!

God is gracious and merciful, slow to anger and great in loving kindness. God is good to all and His mercy is over all His works. God mightiness and kingship is praised and glorified!

Praise God! Praise his Holy name forever!

Living to Impress

When I got up this morning, after prayer, I asked Jesus what would He have me write today. He told me to write about those of us who live to impress others. Why? Why do so many of us live to impress others? Maybe it is because our social environment demands it! We are living in a "status quo" environment. We live in a society that every one has their expectations of how each other should live. Our parents, sister, brother, children, teachers and yes, even our friends. They all have their expectation of what we should be and how we should live.

We are separated by race and religion. We are categorized by being classed as, low class, middle class and higher classed people. Each class of people is expected to perform according to society's views and expectations. The higher classed who are the ruling society expects all others to live according to their laws and do what they consider to be acceptable! It is sad that many of us are victims of what is sociably acceptable. We strive to please mankind instead of God! We want to please, impress and be accepted at whatever cost. I know. Been there, done that to!

I wanted my family to be proud of me. I received a pretty decent education and I seem to always get good of jobs. And yes, I wanted people to look up to me. I wanted them to be impressed with my education, job and of course, my wits and intelligence! Guess what living to please and impress others did for me? It brought to me nothing but misery and unhappiness. For example, when I was living in the world instead of the word. I was living to impress people especially at parties and hanging out! I wanted to fit in. I had to be that fun (everybody loves Audrey!) person. Drinking and getting high!

Yeah, I was the life of the party. I was getting drunk, talking junk and making everyone laugh. And for the most part I was just trying to hang and be accepted. Deep down inside of me, I really was lonely, sad and even lost! I did not know what my purpose in life was. There was something missing in my life for the longest. I just did not know what it was. I did not have any sense of purpose nor direction in my life.

Thank God! I figured it out! I had not lived my life in Christ according to His laws and principles! I was living my life according to mans laws and principles. I was blind to Satans' deceit, living in the world. Duh! I was not aware of what was going on. I was dumb, participating in Satans fun!

I know that I was born into sin and I know that I have done some pretty dumb things. Living to impress was one of the dumb things. Thank God for loving me and opening my eyes. I surrendered my life to Him. I have learned to be sober and vigilant because I know that my adversary is the DEVIL. I know that the Devil is like a roaring lion, walking about, seeking whom he may devour and it is written in 1Peter 5:8-9. And I also know that whoever resists the Devil and be steadfast in faith will know that, the affliction of impressing people is in all those that are in the world.

I realize that you nor I, should live to impress or please man. Society is not our salvation. First of all, society for the most part, is not living according to the laws and principles of God, but a society that is evidently living in Satan world of darkness! To "PLEASE and IMPRESS?" To "impress" is another weapon of Satan.

You can never impress God! But, you can "Please Him!" Why "IMPRESS MAN" when it is easier to "PLEASE GOD!"

From Psalm 37

Don't worry about the wicked. Don't envy those who do wrong.

Trust in the Lord and do good. Then you will live safely in the land and prosper.

Take delight in the Lord and he will give you your heart's desires.

Commit everything you do to the Lord. Trust him and he will help you.

Be still in the presence of the Lord and wait patiently for Him to act. Don't worry about evil people who prosper.

Day by day the Lord takes care of the innocent and they will receive a reward that lasts forever.

They will survive through hard times. Those blessed by the Lord will inherit the land.

The steps of the godly are directed, by the Lord. He delights in every detail of their lives. Though they stumble, they will not fall, for the Lord holds them by the hand.

Audrey F. Evans-Ford

G *rabbing, accepting and*
R *eceiving anything and*
E *verthing, forgetting that*
E *vil one Satan, the*
D *evil himself is a giver, too*

Money, What About It?

I have a cousin that died, because of his desire for money. He was not even a quarter of a century in years of life. In fact, he had just turned twenty-one three months prior to his death. I will never forget his favorite song. In fact we were in route to Atlanta in search of an illegal way to make money. A song came on the radio, and we began to sing along with this song, "I want money, lots and lots of money, I wanna be rich!" and so forth and so on! My young cousin was killed approximately three days later in Atlanta. He was robbed and killed. Is money truly the root of evil? Of course not! Satan is the root of Evil!

Satan has been tempting mankind from the beginning of his rule of this world. He knows what man wants and mans' desire. He also knows what man does not want! He knows that the man that love and possesses the things of the world love money and more than likely, this man is an ungodly man. An ungodly man wants everything given to him without waiting, pain, hard labor and suffering. He wants to obtain it quick and easy taking whatever shortcuts necessary. The shortcut is exactly what Satan wants him to take! Taking the shortcut is coming his way and the money is one of his tools!

Many of us are caught up in the world system. Many of us have become lovers of money, because we want the luxuries of life. Many of us have fallen away from Gods word and His principles for living. We have forgotten about the eternal life that Jesus died for us to have. All we think about is the here and now. We want the things that we can see now. We do not focus on the things that God has promised us, which are unseen. "No Patience, No Faith nor Trust"

Jesus tells us that those of us who are determined to be rich fall into temptation. We get caught in the snare of the Devil and become senseless. Our desires become hurtful and plunges us into destruction and ruin. The love of money is a root of all sorts of injurious things and by reaching out for this love (money) some have been led astray from the faith and have stabbed themselves all over with many pains, this is written in 1Timothy 6:9-10. My young cousin died a violent death. I am not saying that he loved money. He just did not know and trust God to supply his needs. Now my cousin's life has been terminated.

The number one rule about money is this; "You cannot be a slave of God and for Riches" read about it in the book of Luke 12:15. Did you know that a slave for riches is a slave to sin! Jesus assures you that the wages of sin is death. Are you thinking about the after life? Or are you caught in Satan snare, the system of the world?

Guess what? You can live in this world and have all the riches of life without shortcuts (sin). Everything that Satan gives to you, God can give you! In fact God can give to you the things that Satan can't give to you. Example, God can give you everlasting life! All you need to do is have a godly devotion, pursue righteousness and love, be mild tempered, have faith and endure. Fight a good fight of the faith and get a firm hold on the everlasting life you are called to. God will furnish all things richly for your enjoyment and give you everlasting life! This is written in 1Timothy 6:12.

Jesus tells us to "Stop storing up for yourselves treasures upon the earth, where moth and rust consume and where thieves break in and steal. For, where your treasure is, there your heart will be also!" this is written in the book of Matthew 6:19,21. In other words, it is what is in a person's heart that makes money good or evil. Greed for the things of this world is a sin.

Sure many of us want the things of the world that Satan tempts us with. The fun, luxury, lust, partying, Vegas, etc…you know what I mean. This does not make you evil. You do not have to be evil to be a sinner! Many people have been deceived by Satan to believe that there is power in money. Wrong, there's no power in money and therefore money does not give power. Money can't buy love, money can't heal you, money can't save you and money sure can get you into the kingdom of heaven.

Jesus said for us to keep our eyes open and guard against every sort of covetousness, and even when a person has abundance, his life does not result from the things that he possesses, this is in the book of Luke 12:15. Don't Be Greedy! Be obedient! Don't get caught up in the lies and deceit of Satan! Satan is a liar! Don't let him continue to deceive you! Even though you may be a sinner, you can be a "Winner!"

Remember, Jesus is the power and the glory of life everlasting! If you don't know Jesus, get to know him! He has all the riches that you need and could ever want! "Jesus is not a liar" whatever He said that He would do, He will do it! Jesus word will prove to be!

What about money? What is money in relationship with our heart? Think about it, what will your love for money gain you? What will your love for Jesus gain you? I will tell you what I know that money is not! Money is not our "Salvation!"

I am blessed and I am rich. And I am not talking about money. My riches is in Christ Jesus. Thank You Lord!

Audrey F. Evans-Ford

What is Halloween?

It happened on Friday, October the eighth, nineteen ninety- nine. I picked up my eight year old grandson for the weekend. While pulling out of my daughter driveway, out of nowhere my grandson asked me about Halloween. He asked me, "What is Halloween Grandma?" I looked at him surprised and I thought about it before answering him. Then all of a sudden it hit me! Halloween is the celebration of sin honoring Satan and his works!

I had never given any thought to what Halloween really is. It was just a night to go trick or treating, wearing costumes and going to parties. I never thought about what Halloween really was. Just think, it is right there in front of our eyes! And yet, Satan has blinded us with candy, partying and having fun. Satan did real good, he deceived us with CANDY!" Can you believe that we fell into his trap? Well, we did.

I do not know exactly when Halloween actually begun. But I read in Kenneth Copeland's Believers voice of Victory magazine that Halloween stems directly from a Irish, Scottish and British folk custom. It was originally celebrated to honor Samhain, lord of the dead. This celebration was started by a priesthood called Druids. They believed that on October 31, that Samhain called all the wicked souls that had been condemned to live in animal bodies. Yes, this to is the work of Satan!

Think about it, many of us have been blinded by Satan's deceit for many generations. Many of us celebrate Halloween just because of tradition not even giving thought to what we are celebrating or why we are celebrating it. Many people see Halloween just as a night of tricks or treats and dressing up in costumes. Satan is so good that he has businesses advertising His night of celebration "Halloween!"

We decorate for the occasion. We buy candy for the children. We dress the children in costumes and take them trick or treating. The adults go to costume parties, get boozed up and whatever else. Hey it's Halloween, lets have some fun. Some of us do mean things just to make people scream. Some throw parties in cemeteries, disturbing the graves and tombs of the dead. Some wear black and red trying to call back the dead. They play Satan's evil games, doing evil things. Its Halloween, we are just having fun! The celebration of Halloween is the celebration of Satan, the celebration of "Evil!" What is the fun in doing evil? What is the fun in celebrating the work of Satan? Will there be this much fun in Hell!

Open your eyes, can't you see what has been and is going on. We have been caught up in the pleasures and fun in sin. It is true, we were all born into sin, this is a fact. But, this does not mean that we have to live sinful lives. It is written in Hosea 12:7 that "He (Satan) is a merchant, the balances of deceit are in his hand: he loves to oppress." Satan is good at what he does. His trickery got you to celebrate "Halloween" the night that you willfully celebrate his evilness and sin against our Father God!

I know that many of you do not see celebrating Halloween as a sin, nor do you see it as being a sin or wrong. You have been blinded, but you need to regain your sight. You need to put on your thinking cap and remember what God said in Matthew 6:24 that "No man can serve two masters. For you will hate one and love the other. You cannot serve both God and mammoth." Think about it. Who will you serve, Satan (Halloween and Hell) or God (Eternal Life in His Kingdom)?

Thank you "Scoop" for asking me "What is Halloween?" thank you Jesus for opening my eyes!

Cleanliness and Clearness

"We need software to clean the cluttered attic of our minds." This is a statement made by Ellen Goodman. Goodman is trying to introduce this BH99 idea as a program for computers. Goodman speaks about her concept of the human brain. She speaks about how the brain obtains and stores so much knowledge that it becomes cluttered. She feels that if our brains had the function of a computer we could do away with any knowledge or thoughts that we no longer care to have. "Clean out the attics of our minds."

I understand what she is saying, but in all reality it is a horrible idea! The reason I say this is because, think about it, just suppose you could take whatever thoughts and memories that you choose and put them on a disc, which ones would you store on the disc?

Okay, you decide to store all bad memories and experiences on the disc. You do not want these things in your mind anymore. Having the technology to do this, you put it on a disc and then delete it. Guess what, now you have no knowledge or memory of those bad times or the lessons learned. Have you ever heard it said, "We learn from our experiences and mistakes?" Well, you cannot learn from something that you know nothing about. Remember, you stored it on the disc and deleted it!

In all of my stories I tell you to "Watch out for Satan" the Bible tells you in Hosea 12:7 that Satan "He is a merchant, and the balance of deceit are in his hands; he love to oppress." In 1 Peter 5:8 we are told to "Be careful! Watch out for attacks from the Devil!" he is our greatest enemy and a liar!

Could this idea of Ms. Goodman be a thought, an idea planted in her mind by Satan. Is this another trick of Satan's to destroy Gods children and mankind?

Suppose we could store bad memories and experiences on a disc and delete them. Then one morning we wake up with a cluttered mind and decided to store some 'not so important' thoughts and memories on a disc. We are just going to store them, not delete them. We are making room for more important things. Now in making our selection of what we are going to store, we decide to store our Bible knowledge. We decide to do this because we have Jesus in our hearts.

Acknowledge, Beware and Recognize

We feel that because we know that we love Jesus and He loves us, it is okay to store our Bible knowledge on a disc. It is okay and its safe.

Is it really okay and is it really safe? Remember, Satan is on his job! You! You are his job and he is working diligently and faithfully on you. Think about it, you have stored your knowledge and memories of the Bible on a disc and this stored information accidentally gets deleted. Now, do you still love Jesus? How can you? You have no knowledge of Him! Was it really an accident that the knowledge and memory of Jesus was deleted? Or was it the work of Satan?

Modern technology and the comforts of luxury have made it difficult for many of us to think of our lives in spiritual terms. We do not take time out to spend quality time with God. Sure, many of us pray and give thanks. But, I am here to tell you this is not enough! God deserves better from us. He deserves more from us than what we are giving Him. Look at what God has given to us, His only begotten Son, our Lord and Savior Jesus Christ!

The bottom line is this, "We are all Gods children" He made us, He created us and He is the one that sustain us each morning. Every breath that we take is because of God. Man cannot create nor recreate Gods work. We need to establish a spiritual foundation and spend more quality time with God.

Is Ms. Goodmans idea aided by implanted thoughts from the god of this world? Being able to store our knowledge and memories on a disc is truly food for thought!

There is one very important things that we must do in reference to Ms. Goodmans idea and that is to acknowledge, beware, recognize and watch out for Satan! "Stay on Guard with God!"

If you feel that your mind is cluttered and needs to be Cleaned and Cleared out. Here is a suggestion, "Soak in the Word of God!"

Audrey F. Evans-Ford

We Can Stop This "Madness"

As parents, we have an obligation and responsibility to God and our children. When we have children, we have been blessed, because we have been given guardianship of Gods little ones. And we are not only obligated, but we are also responsible for raising them according to God's laws and principles.

I feel pretty safe saying that I do believe that many of us were brought up in Christian Homes and raised up according to the laws and principles of God. However, many of us have fallen and have been caught in the snare of the Devil. We have become worldly people instead of being holy and godly people. We do many things that we know are wrong and are sinful, yet we continue to do them.

Today, many parents do not have time to raise their children. Why? Because they are to busy. They are trying to keep bread on the table and live in luxury. They work many hours and do not having time for their children. The children are turned over to babysitters, nannies, daycares, etc... Many of these parents when asked why do they work so hard and so many hours they reply by saying that they want the best for their children. They want to give to their children the things that they did not have. I understand this. I am a parent also! But, does this mean that we should not give our children the things that we did have, such as quality time.

This scheme of Satan has caused division in the family. Keeping the parents wanting for more and working longer hours. Keeping them out of touch with God and the children. Each new generation of parents seem to fall farther and farther away from the Church. I was guilty of this myself. I was not living according to Gods principles either. I took God, my children and my life for granted!

We often get caught up in the rushing, rush, rush world and forget about God. We have often forgotten that if it had not been for God, our existence would not be. 'STOP!' Lord Jesus please remind us of how brief our time here is. All this rushing that we are doing is another one of Satan tactics to keep us distracted from you!

Do you realize how many babies are put into daycares almost immediately after they are born? The parents are working all the time and the mothers do not have the time to properly nurture their infants. Then we have parents who take a break every now and then and spend a little time with their children and they complain that their children just won't listen. Our children are to be instructed to be obedient. It is written in Ephesians 6:4-6 "And you fathers, (parents) do not provoke your children to wrath, but bring them up in the training and admonition (mental-regulating) of the Lord." It is also written in Proverbs 22:6 that if we train up our children in the way they should go, when they are older they will not depart from it. But, how can we as parents teach them about God, His laws and principles if we do not have time for them?

The problems with children have become so great that parents seek knowledge from therapist and sociologist about how to raise their them. Then we have doctors prescribing medication for children, who do not act according to the norm. Whatever that is! What's wrong with children laughing and playing and running and making noise? I did those things when I was a child and you probably did them too! But, today when children rip and run, they are hyper and need medication.

Parents we need to take time and see what is really going on. The only Doctor that we need for our children and ourselves is Jesus! Jesus said, "Let the young children alone and do not hinder them; do not hinder them from coming to Him for the kingdom of heaven belongs to suchlike ones" this is written in the book of Matthew 19:14. As Christians and parents we need to open our eyes and see what is and has happened.

Why do you really work long hours? Why do our children spend more time in daycares and after school care then they do with you? What is it that you really want out of this life so much, that you are willing to sacrifice your children's up bringing and eternal life with God?

While you think about it, think about this, "Satan has deceived you once again." Satan can't give you anything that God can't! In fact, Satan can't give to you the things that God can! In Matthew 6:19-20 Jesus said, "Stop storing up treasure for ourselves on earth and store treasures for ourselves in heaven. Jesus told us that God clothes the vegetation of the field, which is here today and tomorrow is thrown into the oven, will our Father not much rather clothe us? We have so little faith in our Father!

Tie a string around your finger if you have to, remember that our children are a blessing from God, with a job. Our job is to raise the children in the word of God. We are responsible for teaching them the laws and principles of God. Our job is to also teach the children to live accordingly! I will tell you this; working for God is the highest paying job that you will ever have! Raise the children in the "Word" and get paid! Receive the bonus! "**Heaven!**"

It is written in the book of Hebrews 5:12 that we ought to be teachers, but in view of the time, we again need someone to teach us from the beginning the elementary things of the scared pronouncements of God. Our Father know that we have been bitten by the evil serpent and He has given us the "Antidote" to stop this madness! His "WORD!" "USE IT!"

We Must Save Our Children

In New York, growing up, my sister and I have a girlfriend, who has a younger sister. Her sister is about ten years younger than we are. And we were about thirteen and fourteen, no more than fifteen years old at the time. Our friends little sister was truly a brat. You wanted to just simply kill her. But, we loved her bad and all. One day this child just kept on doing crazy, naughty, just bad things.

Well there was an older woman who lived in the household with this child and everyone called her 'Aunt Annie" even our parents. One day our friends little sister was misbehaving and every time Aunt Annie would say something to her about her behavior, she would scream and holler and say that the Devil made her do it. So, Aunt Annie took her and held her in her arms and rubbed prophet oil on her forehead and began to pray in Jesus name for the Devil to leave the little girl alone. We thought, yeah, right! We laughed and joked about it. Today, I wonder if the little girl was really telling the truth!

I thought about this incident after reading an article in the Sun Newspaper about eleven year old twins shooting their mother and sister and killing their father. The headline is what caught my eyes. It read, "Mom tells friend they were not My Sons" and then the wheels in my head started turning. I thought about the movie "The Stand" a Stephen King movie. I thought about the nightly news that followed the movie that night. There were Priests on the news being interviewed about demons. The Priests acknowledged the existence of demons and that they are here among us, now.

Oh yeah, it is true. I know from personal experience. No, I am not pulling your leg. Yes, demons entered my mind and body through drugs and alcohol. And they took control over of my mind and over my body. I watched a demon come out of me and harmed my husband, whom I love with all my heart. I thank God today for His divine intervention! I saw Gods' hand shield David's face from what could have been fatal and a physically scared for life situation. I threw hot grease into my husbands face. As the grease was being dashed out of the pot into David's face, I saw the hand of God shield and protect his face. I could see clear through the hand that was shielding his face, and the cross that David wore and wears around his neck glowed like a shining sun of gold! It was very bright! That night I saw the demon and I saw God's hand. Oh, I know that demons exist and yes they are real. It is written in 1 Peter 5:8 that Jesus said for us to "Be careful and watch out for the Devil!" So watch out! They are real and they do exist!

Let me tell you, after that encounter with the demon, I hurried without lingering to call on Jesus. Begging and pleading asking Jesus to please forgive me and to help me! I have done a lot of mean and dumb things, but this one took the cake! To me, this was the worst thing that I had ever done. I let a demon, take control over my mind and body, using me to do what it wanted me to do and I could not stop it. I wanted to but I couldn't! Whew! is all I can say. But I will tell you this, if I have to be controlled by any spirit, I much rather be controlled by the Holy Spirit of God!

I always thought that demons just bothered older people. I see that Satan is ruthless! He does not discriminate. Age makes no difference. An eleven year old girl killed her thirteen month old cousin. Eleven year old twins killed their father. Two middle school girls, both twelve years old, fought on a school bus. One girl choked another girl until she was unconscious and was still continually being hit and beating. Twenty year young man was killed by a seventeen year old. These are just a few of the violent acts committed by children in the State of South Carolina.

There are children all over the state, the nation and the world that are committing violets acts. Yes, demons exist in our children too! It is written in Hebrews 2:14 that the young children are sharers of blood and flesh, they also similarly partook of the same things, that through Jesus death he might bring to nothing the one having the means to cause death! And that is the Devil!

We have to take back our children and protect them from Satan and his demons. It is written in 2 Chronicles 30:9 that "If we return to the Lord, our brethren and our "Children" will be treated with compassion by those who lead them captive, so that they may come back into the land; for the Lord our God is gracious and merciful. Believe it! God will not turn His face away from you nor your children, if you return to Him!

Therefore, do what we are told to do in Ephesians 6:11, "put on the complete suit of armor from God that we maybe able to stand firm against the machinations of the Devil, Satan himself! We can save our children by turning from sin and living according to the laws and principles of Gods.

Come on, why let Satan take our lives and the lives of our children, we can be saved and we can "Save Our Children"

Audrey F. Evans-Ford

A Book for All Children

I read an article in the Greenville News about a group of parents objecting to an award-winning novel having been selected for their children to read. The children were to read the book over the summer and be tested on the book when school resumed.

Well the parents did not find anything rewarding in this award-winning novel. These parents complained about the depicting sex abuse scenes in this book. One scene is an eight year old little girl, who is the main character, waking up in bed with her mothers boyfriend and is sexually abused. The parents were very upset about this type of book being selected for their children to read.

The parents being upset went to the school board about it. The school board found this novel to be an interesting book to read. One of the parents became very angry about that statement and she told the school board that if giving her child a book with depicting sex abuse scenes is what they call interesting, then "Bore my children!" She told the school board "Don't go and pick a book that is this graphic because you are afraid my kids will be bored in school."

After reading this article, I thought about what those parents were saying, and my thoughts went farther. I thought about how our children are allowed to read just about any type of book in school that they want to. Now they are being 'REQUIRED' to read books with depicting sex scenes.

Wow! What Gaul Satan has! He has had prayer taken out of the school and replaced it with books of depicting sex scenes. Thank God for the parents that stand up for their rights and the rights of their children! Thank God that parents have a right and a say in what our children read. This article brought about a question that I have had for quite sometime, if our children are required to read sex depicting books and fairy tales, then why are they not required to read the "Bible?" Oh, I already know why, I just want to know if you know. It is the work of Satan.

Satan is a liar and is always deceiving the children of God. He started his work in the schools when he had prayer thrown out! What you did not know is that it was Satan's work. Satan knew way back

Acknowledge, Beware and Recognize

when, that prayer at home was strong in the family and to pray away from home other than Church had to be stopped. So he stopped prayer in the schools.

Yeah, I know. It is this thing about religious rights and imposing your religion on others. Hello! Wake up! What difference does it make if there is prayer in the school or not? After all, People are going to believe what they want to believe and listen to what they want to hear. So, who is it really hurting if prayer is in the schools? The children or Satan? Think about it!

Don't you see what Satan is doing? Satan wants our children and he will stop at nothing to get them. See how he has is manipulated the system with his lies and deceit! In Daniel 1:4 it is written that we are reminded to see that our "children in whom there was no defect at all, but good in appearance and having insight into all wisdom and being acquainted with knowledge," the knowledge of God! We need to make the "Bible" a required book to be read in school.

The Bible has such wonderful stories, Adam and Eve, Noah and the Ark, The Parting of the Red Sea, The Ten Commandments, Jonah and The Whale, John the Baptist, The Birth of Jesus, The Life of Jesus, How Jesus feed million with five loaves of bread and two fish, How Jesus healed the sick, raised the dead, made a blind man see and the cripple man walk, How Jesus cast our demons etc... The stories in the Bible are endlessly, fulfilling and rewarding. The Bible is informative and holds all truths. The Bible is the book of life and truth. The Bible is God's will for our lives and the lives of our children!

It is written in John 17:3 that "until we all attain to the oneness in the faith and in the accurate knowledge of the Son of God we will not measure in stature the fullness of Christ." And of course Satan does not want us to do that!

Parents must continue to take a stand and an interest in what our children are reading in school.

Parents, we must Kick "SATAN" out of school! We must always take a stand for God! Educate the children in the word of Our Father!

Audrey F. Evans-Ford

"BEWARE AND KNOW"

Contradictive

Okay, what am I talking about now? "The Bible" I am talking about the Bible. I do not know about you, but I have heard it said many times that the Bible is contradictive. Well during the time I would hear it being said, it did not matter to me if the Bible was contradictive or not. I did not put thought into that statement one way or the other. I was living in the world, so call enjoying my life partying, getting hi and doing other things. Oh and I was not reading the Bible and I was not thinking about reading it! So, how would I know if the Bible was contradictive or not?

Well, after so many years of falls, scrapes and bruises in my life, I gave up! I called on Jesus and I started reading the Bible. Thank God, I had a little bit of knowledge, enough to call on Jesus! In James 4:8-10 the Bible says, "Draw nigh to God, and He will draw nigh to you. Cleanse your hands, ye sinners; and purify your hearts, ye double-minded." I knew it was time for me to come in and draw closer to God! I had become as it is told in James 4:8-10, I had become afflicted with mourning and weeping: and all my laughter had been turned to mourning, and all my joy turned to heaviness." I knew what I had to do, I had to do what James 4:8-10 says, I had to "Humble (myself) yourselves in the sight of the Lord, and he shall lift you up!" And that is exactly what I did. I humbled myself before the Lord. Praise God! He lifted me up!

I had taken my niece Trinessa to the dentist one day, and after we left the dentist we had to go get her prescription filled. While I waited for her to get her prescription filled. I stayed in the car reading the word of God. In the back of my testament there is a section of the book that said, "Touch Points for New Christians" and of course I began to read it. I came to a question in this section that asks, "Does God always answer prayers?" This question was asked in reference to what happened to Apostle Paul, one of Jesus disciples. It said that,

"God answers prayer by giving us "not what we ask" for but, something better." Yes, God always answer our prayers!

I was like, oh no, I don't want to hear that! That is not what I read in the Bible. I got a bit huffy about this statement because that is not what Jesus told me in the Bible. Jesus said whatsoever that I ask in His name that it shall be given to me! So, I was not about to hear anything about not giving to me what I ask for, but something better. Then it start setting in, yeah the Bible is contradictive. I want exactly what I ask for. And that's that!

Guess what happened to me at that point? The Holy Spirit stepped in and like always He was right on time. He stepped in and kicked Satan out of the car and filled me with wisdom and knowledge. He showed me how that lying, deceitful, Devil does not give up! People that make statements referring to the Bible as being contradictive evidently do not know Jesus! When you get to know Jesus, on an intimate level, you will know that there is nothing and I mean absolutely nothing contradictive about the Bible.

To say that the Bible is contradictive is to offend and dishonor God. It is also calling God a liar! This is blasphemy! The word "contradictive" belongs to Satan the one that tries to infiltrate our minds with his lies. My definition for contradictive is:

CON: Satan himself!
CONTRA: Satan device to control!
DICTIVE: Satan deceit!

Satan is trying to put it into our minds that the Bible is contradictive hoping that we will get upset and angry enough to put the Bible down and never pick it up again.

When people would refer to the Bible as being contradictive they would say something like this, "God says that if some one slaps your face, then turn and give to them the other cheek. And yet, God turns around and says an eye for an eye." Believe me, there is nothing contradictive about these statements. It is all in how you perceive them! This is why we are told in the Bible in the Book of Proverbs 3:5-6 to "Trust in the Lord with all your heart, and lean not to your own understanding; but in all your ways acknowledge Him and He shall direct your path." So, stop leaning to your own understanding and get to know Jesus on a personal and intimate level. Then you will know what these statements mean.

It is written in the book of Matthew 5:38-39 that Jesus says, "You have heard that it was said, 'An eye for and eye and a tooth for a tooth.' But, I tell you not to resist an evil person. But whoever slaps you on your right cheek, turn the other to him also." Jesus was saying, repay evil with goodness. Try it the next time some one decides to slap you. No, I am not crazy and I am serious.

Think about it. Someone slaps you and you do not strike back. I can almost guarantee you that the sting to your face will leave quicker than the thought in their mind as to why you did not strike them back. They will be wondering what are you up to? What are you going to do? Oh, they will be totally confused and wondering if you are going to do anything at all?

Number two, an eye for an eye does not mean if someone pluck out your eye for you to go pluck theirs out too! Jesus says love thy enemy. Jesus never taught violence! Jesus is the Prince of Peace!

Look, Satan wants you to believe that the Bible is contradictive so that you will not only doubt the word of God, but that you will eventually not longer believe the word of God, nor His promises!

But, remember what I have been telling you! Satan is more than a liar, he is our greatest adversary and enemy!

No the Bible is not contradictive and yes, Jesus always answers our prayers. And yes it is what we ask, and yes it is better than what we ask, because Jesus wants to always give to us the BEST!

Jesus always give to you what you ask. He just simply makes it better! Jesus gives to you the best because you are heir to all that belong to Him and our Father. Can you say the same thing about yourself? Do you give Jesus your best?

There is nothing contradictive about the Bible. Jesus word is firm in heaven and will never returns void! Rebuke Satan! Recognize Satan lies and deceit! You know that Satan he is out to destroy us! Watch Out For The Lies And Deceit Of:

"THE CON ARTIST- SATAN!"

Selfishness

One Sunday I went to Church with a friend. I went to Church with her because she spoke with such admiration for the Pastor there, that I wanted to hear his sermon and to meet him. She spoke of how wonderful you feel during and after his service. She spoke of how "Spirited Up Lifted" you are when he has spoken the word of God! This was exactly how I wanted to feel! Glory to God! This is how I felt after his sermon!

Being a visitor, I was given a card to fill out. My girlfriend and I were the last people to enter into the temple. This made us the last ones to fill out the visitor cards. Well at the end of the service, the Pastor thanked and welcomed the visitors by calling their names. Lo and be hold, he called my name first! This to me was a blessing and God telling me that he was and is always with me! Yes, I think like this at times. You see, sometimes we need a visible sign of Gods presences and availability. Please do not misunderstand me. I know that God is always with me. God understands me and know my needs and this is why He makes it known that He is with me!

Getting back to the sermon, the sermon was about debt. Well the first thing that came to my mind was money. A money debt, you are broke and owe everyone. Guess what? I was off base. The debt that the Pastor was speaking of was, being in debt to God! When he asked how many of us were in debt to God, I knew right away what he was talking about. I lifted my hands in praise and admitted that I am in debt to God! The Pastor proceeded to explain what the debt to God is. The debt to God is when He blesses you with knowledge and wisdom of His word and you do not pass it on.

The Bible tells us in Galatians 5:13 that we have been called together in liberty by love to serve one another. For all the law is fulfilled in one word, even in this; "Thou shalt love thy neighbor as thyself." Loving your neighbor is more than sharing your homes, food or money. Loving one another is sharing the word of God! Pattie LaBelle sings about passing on your blessings in her song, "When You've Been Blessed" she says, "Pass it on!" Thank you Pattie

LaBelle, Thank you God for her beautiful voice! Yes, God wants us to pass His blessing on! Believe me He has more in store for us.

After hearing the sermon about debt, I realized that I really had not been passing my blessings. I was in debt. I owe God! Oh, I had been paying my debt in dribbles and bits, while God was still yet blessing me abundantly. I honestly did not realize that I was being selfish. I thought that I was doing something because I was praying. I realize now that I was blinded by Satan and I could not see that I was being selfish, even in my prayers. But, our Father bought it to my attention in this sermon! The sermon was for me!

Thank you Father God! The message to me did not stop there. On the way home from church I was listening to the radio and the disc jockey played a song by the Eastcoast Choir, "Lord Touch Somebody." The lyrics in the song was asking God to bless somebody, because there is someone in need of a blessing. Behold, the Lord was speaking to me again!

The message from God to me was confirmed in the song! I did not realize that I had been being selfish, but I will tell you this, I am "**not selfish**" anymore! I pass my blessings on! I thank God for giving to me wisdom and knowledge! And now I strive to be debt "**Free!**"

My Addiction

I understand addiction to be a bad habit. An addiction and a bad habit are both damaging. Most people when talking about bad habits are talking about such things as, smoking cigarettes, biting nails, sucking thumbs, etc... and when they speak of addiction, they are usually talking about the use or need for drugs, alcohol, pills, gambling, sex, etc... all which are tools of the Devil and they are damaging and harmful to both the mind and the body. I had both, the bad habits and the addictions. One of my bad habits was smoking cigarettes. My so called addiction was smoking crack cocaine. They "WERE" bad. Thank God I am set free!

I suffered so much hurt and pain because of so called addiction and my bad habits that I gave up and gave my life to Christ. I decided to give up my life in the world. The world belongs to Satan, so I gave up my life in Satans' world and stopped living in sin. I stopped doing what the elders use to call, ripping and running in the streets and I stopped using drugs and smoking cigarettes. I had issues that I was running from. Guess what? All the running that I did, all I was doing was running in a circle, not going anywhere.

In Psalm 51:5-6 it says that "I was born a sinner – yes, from the moment my mother conceived me. But, God desire honesty from the heart, so He can teach me to be wise in my inmost being." This is when I realized that I belong to God. I surrendered my life to Jesus and let Him have His way in me and with me. It is because of Jesus I know that even though I was born into sin, I do not have to live in sin! And neither do you! Praise God!

Satan tries to convince you that since you were born into sin that you must live in it and die in it! Satan is a liar! Yeah! Satan had his death choke (crack cocaine) on my throat and tried to put me in the grave! Praise Be to God! Jesus saved me! I saw only trouble and sorrow (losing all those who I love). Then I called Jesus! Please Lord Jesus, save me! How kind the Lord is! So merciful is our Father! God protects all of us with childlike faith. I was surely facing death and Jesus saved me! Try it, give your life to Jesus and watch how your life will change. He will open your eyes to see the wickedness in the world, (remember the "WORLD" belongs to Satan.) Jesus will open your ears to hear His voice and fill your heart with love. Jesus will also give to you wisdom and knowledge! He did it for me and He will do it for you.

Listen, drugs had become a major issue in my life that I had to face! They had become a serious problem in my life and I am here to tell that you cannot solve a problem until you recognize the problem. Right? Therefore, speaking of people with bad habits and addictions, if they are in denial, this means they do not realize nor except that they have a problem, then there is no solution, because there is no problem. But, when one admits to him or herself that there is a problem, then submission to the problem begin stops! This is what I did. I recognized that I had a problem with drugs and I faced it! I called Jesus into my life and I stopped denying that I had a problem with drugs and then my submission to drugs stopped. I am not going to let the Devil nor his drugs do anymore damage to my life

I can still remember all the bad, hurtful, sad and depressing times during my drug use and how I cried and called Jesus. Promising if He get me out of this and give me a new life, I would stay away from the drugs and do only His will. Guess What? Jesus answered me and helped me just like He promised He would. He gave me a new life, joy and peace. He even gave to me my hearts desire. But, still I would stumble and fall, time and time again. A yet, He was still there, picking me up, answering my prayers, giving to me my hearts desire and blessing me every time! Not once had Jesus ever said no to me! Not once did Jesus fail me. Not once did Jesus forsake me!

This is when I realized that Jesus Christ is my addiction too! Yes, I used and abused Him too. Let me explain this in a little more depth. Some drug addicts experience physical pain for drugs because their body needs it. Thank you Jesus! I am blessed, I have never had this experience. I had never had a craving for drugs and my body never suffered any pain for the need of drugs. My drug use was a mental thing. I believe this to be true in many cases, with many drug users. That it is a mental thing. The "THINK" they are addicts think that they need the drugs. I learned from Joyce Meyers that "Were the Mind Goes," the man will follow!

Jesus has been my addiction all along. I just did not know it at the time I was using drugs. My savior has made me to listen and to see. I used Him like I used drugs. And Jesus loves me so much, that He let me use Him as a drug. Oh Praise God! Whenever I had a problem I called on Jesus and He came and took away all my pain! The difference in Jesus being my drug instead of crack cocaine is that the "Hi" with Jesus lasts forever and it's free. The "Hi" with drugs is temporary and it cost much more than money!

Yes, I am an addict! I am addicted to Jesus and I am not giving up this addiction. I do not want to recover from this addiction, not at all! To an Addict that may be reading this, I say to you "put your money back in your pockets" call Jesus! In fact, I dare you, no I double dare you to take a chance, the next time you decide to get Hi, get Hi with Jesus.

If you have read this, then believe every word that you have just read. Because if it had not been for Jesus, you would not have read these words! Yes, My addiction is Jesus! Praise God, Thank You Jesus!

Audrey F. Evans-Ford

Words of Comfort and Strength Psalm 34

At all times praise the Lord, boasting only in Him exalting His name. For those who look to Him for help will be radiant with joy and no shadow of shame will darken their faces.

Let the Lord's people show Him reverence, for those who love and honor Him will have all they need. The Lord hears His people when they call to Him for help. He rescues them from all their troubles. The Lord is close to the brokenhearted; He rescues those who are crushed in spirit.

The righteous face many troubles, but the Lord rescues them from each and every one. The Lord protects them from harm, not one of their bones will be broken! Even strong young lions sometimes go hungry, but those who trust in the Lord will never lack any good thing.

The eyes of the Lord watch over those who do right; His ears are open to their cries for help. Turn away from evil and do good. Work hard at living in peace with others. Watch your tongue! Keep your lips from telling lies!

The Lord will redeem those who serve Him. Everyone who trusts in Him will be freely pardoned. I prayed and cried out to the Lord in my suffering and He heard me, He answered me freeing me from all my fears. Taste and see that the Lord is good. Oh, the joys of those who trust in Him.

Love and trust God with all your heart. God loves you and He hears you. He will not fail you! He will help you, healing you and giving to you your hearts desire. God is not a liar! Turn from evil and try to do good. God even blesses you for trying!

Tough Love

I, like so many people that have or have had serious problems, felt that I needed help from the ones that were closest to me. Well they were there for me and they tried to help me. But, nothing was changing so they decided to show me tough love. Let me also state this, my problem was basically the same problem over and over again, "Drugs!" And those who were close to me, simply just got feed up! I can understand this and I respect this. Most of all, I still love them. They never gave up, they just gave out! They gave out of tolerance and patience. They did not give out of Love!

One night, I could not sleep and I was thinking about the tough love that I had been shown during a time I was so afraid and felt alone. I thought that I was losing my mind and I was thinking that I was not going to make it. Thanks be to God and His mercy, I made it through the tough times. Thank you Lord Jesus for healing me!

Now, on the subject of "Tough Love" I gave plenty of thought to this. Who came up with this thing called, "Tough Love?" I know for sure that it is not the will or the word of God! Therefore, this was an idea planted into mans mind and hearts through the work of Satan. Yes, it is another one of Satan lies to destroy mankind and take their souls.

It is written in the book of Matthew 5:7 "Happy are the merciful, since they will be shown mercy!" And in James 2:13 it is says, "For the one that does not practice mercy will have judgment without mercy. Mercy exults triumphantly over judgment." I really do understand many people who call themselves showing their loved ones tough love. They honestly believe that they are doing something good. This is a lie of Satan deceiving them! Tough love is not mercy!

I believe that many victims that have committed suicide did it because they were being shown "Tough Love." They were weak, afraid and vulnerable. The ones that they loved had turned on them (so they thought) therefore they felt as though they had nothing and no one to live for. They gave up living and gave their lives to Satan because they were deceived by his lies! They were so blinded by

Satan lies that they did not realize that God never stopped loving them and He was waiting for them to call Him.

Listen to me, no matter how great or small your sin may be, no matter how small or great your problem may be, no such thing as "Tough Love" should ever be shown or given. Just who is man that he should be tough on anyone? I thank God that He is God! I thank God that He is my Father, my redeemer, my judge and jury! Our Father God is a God of acts of love, grace, mercy, forgiveness and compassion! Our Father is slow to anger and He is abundant in loving-kindness.

Our Father disciplines us because we are His children. He is not tough on us. He is compassionate, understanding and merciful! I am living proof of Gods love, compassion, understanding and mercy. God has redeemed me, forgiven me for my sins and given to me grace. My Father has shown me favor, He has given me life and He is forever blessing me!

God is merciful and He will cover our error and not bring to us ruin. Many times God makes His anger turn back. God will not raise up in anger. God said that He shall be merciful to our unrighteous deeds and He shall by no means call our sins to mind ever again. This is written in the book of Hebrews 8:12.

In Timothy 1 chapter 1:13, Timothy tells us that, "Although he formerly was a blasphemer and a persecutor and an insolent man. Nevertheless, God showed him mercy because he was ignorant and acted with a lack of faith! It says in Psalm 86:15 "Oh God, you are a God of mercy and grace, slow to anger and abundant in loving-kindness and trueness.

To those of you who have been mislead to believe that it is right to show your loved ones "Tough Love" please know and recognize that this is a lie. This is not the will or the word of God our Father. This is a lie of Satan. I am telling you, if you know some one that may be suffering, in pain and have a problem that is hard for you to deal with, pray for them, don't give up on them, show them mercy, be compassionate and pray for their salvation.

Our Father wants us to show love, compassion, understanding and most of all "MERCY" as He has shown us all! Our Father tells us in Luke 6:36 to "Continue becoming merciful, just as He has been merciful to us!

Remember In James 2:13 it is written that "The one that does not practice mercy will have (his) judgment without mercy! This is the word of God! **Gods word and faithfulness extends to every generation**, as enduring as the earth He created. **God laws remain true today**, everything serves His plans! "Forever, O Lord your word stands firm in heaven!" Psalm 119:89

"TOUGH LOVE OR MERCY?"

"The Choice is Yours!"

Audrey F. Evans-Ford

My Special Prayer from Psalms 38 & 39

Oh Lord my days are filled with grief. I am bent over and racked with pain. My wounds fester and stink because of my foolish sins and my heart is broken. My loved ones and friends stay away from me. They stand at a distance.

Lord Jesus I have confessed my sins; and I am truly sorry for what I have done. Forgive me Lord! Do not abandon me. Don't rebuke me in your rage! Lord when you discipline your people for their sins, their lives can be crushed like the life of a moth. Oh Lord my God, Please don't punish me anymore. My heart beats wildly and my strength is failing. I am on the verge of collapse, facing constant pain.

Lord I pray and ask of thee; "Don't let Satan and my enemies gloat over me and rejoice at my downfall." Lord Jesus do not stand at a distance come quick and help me. Don't ignore my tears. Spare me that I can smile again.

Lord I know my days are numbered and my life is fleeing away. I know my life is no longer than the width of my hand and that an entire lifetime is just a moment to you. Please don't punish me anymore. Hear my prayer and listen to my cries for your help.

My only hope is in your unfailing love and faithfulness. Lord don't hold back your tender mercies from me. Come quick, rescue me, help me, spare me before I exist no more. Let me live and smile again!

The Agony

All through this book I speak to you about trusting in the Lord Christ. I am telling you that He will answer your prayers. Jesus said, in Luke 11:9 to "keep on asking and you will be given what you ask for. Keep on looking and you will find. Keep on knocking and the door will be opened. For everyone who asks receives, everyone who seeks find. And the door is open to everyone who knocks." Jesus said that He would do it and will do it! Jesus word will not return to Him void! I know it for a fact!

I have titled this particular story "The Agony" because when you have decided to give up your life in the world for Jesus, you become impatient waiting for His promises to manifest. You feel now that you have decided to turn your life around and give up sin that Jesus should answer your prayers immediately. Where are your patients? Jesus waited patiently for you. And not once did he complain. Oh the pain of waiting! Think of the pain that Jesus suffered for our sins, up on the cross! And still He patiently waits for us to come to Him.

We say to ourselves "Jesus said that if I ask Him for what I want that He will give it to me." Of course He said it. And yes, I assure you that Jesus meant it. But, because you are impatient, you are in agony because you don't want to wait on the Lord to act in His time. You want Him to act when you say act! In Hebrew 10:36-37 we are told that we "have need of patience and after we have done the will of God, we will receive the promise. In a little while He that shall come will come and will not tarry." So the Bible tells us in Isaiah 1:19 that "If we be willing and obedient, we shall eat the good of the land." Jesus gave His word. So how dare we rush Him!

I know that sometimes we become frustrated and aggravated waiting. Being impatient causes us to be in agony and pain. We want our prayers answered "ASAP" like in yesterday. Then there is the agony of the prayer of "it is going to take a miracle" to be answered. No problem. Jesus is a miracle worker. He made the blind see, the cripple walk and raised the dead. Let me tell you if Jesus said that He will do it, then it is done! The word of God is firm in heaven and on earth. And Gods faithfulness extends to every generation including this one. God has not changed!

The agony that you are feeling is the agony of your past, the agony of how you lived in the world as a sinners among sinners. And what you are also feeling is fear. You fear Gods judgment because you know that you have been wrong. You know that you have been living in sin being disobedient to the word of God. And yes, you do fear Gods' judgment! God is loving, compassionate and understanding! He loves you! He gave His only begotten Son, so that you and I may have eternal life in His kingdom. Sure God gets angry with us sometimes. We have made Him angry many times, and many times in His mercy He has forgiven us! We are forgiven again and again and again! Think about it!

Our agony comes from not having patients and little to no faith. We have lived in the world of sin for so long, that we do not have faith, trust or patients about anything. But, we have realized that nothing that we do lasts for long or work out. In fact everything that we do turns out to be a disaster. Then we remember Jesus! We remember His promises and His works of wonder. Now, we want to give our lives to Jesus, expecting Him to jump when we say jump! It is like we are saying to Jesus "look here, I have decided to turn my life over to you, now here is what I want you to do and I want it done now. SORRY! It does not work that way.

Jesus waited for you, now you have to wait for Him! Yes, He will answer you prayers, giving to you what you ask. But, you must first be obedient to His word and live according to His principles. Trust and have faith in Him. Then in time you will see that your prayers have already been answered. It is written in Hebrew 11:16 that Faith is the substance of things hoped for and the evidence of things not seen. Without faith it is impossible to please God. When you come to God you must believe that He is God and that He is a Rewarder of all those that diligently seek Him.

Last but not least, your "AGONY" is coming from Satan! Satan is determined to destroy you and has targeted your mind by placing doubt in it. He is making you feel guilty and think that your sin is an unforgivable sin. Satan is antagonizes you with thoughts of doubt and fear trying to make you disbelieve God and give up!

Don't do it! Let your "Agony" be your strength. Think about it this way, when you were of the world and things seems to be

Acknowledge, Beware and Recognize

wonderful and yet, they turned out to be a disaster. It was the agony of the hurt and pain of your disasters that turned you to Jesus! It weakened you and brought you to your knees. Okay, so make this agony work for you in a positive way. Use this agony for your strength and be strong believing in the power of God.

It is said in the Bible in 1 Peter 4:16 that "if any man suffer as a Christian, your suffering (agony) is not because of your past, it is because of your future in Christ, meaning that you now are suffering in behalf of Jesus! Don't be ashamed; but be glorify by God in this behalf." Stick with Jesus! He is the miracle worker, the forgiver of sins, and the healer of all your pain and AGONY!

Don't you let Satan stop you from receiving! Keep on Praying, Keep your faith and trust in Jesus! Jesus has already answered your prayers! Patients Please! There is no need for the Agony!

Audrey F. Evans-Ford

Why Do I Cry?

Nations are at war with one another.

Great earthquakes are all around the world – causing much destruction.

Epidemics and famine are swallowing lives by the billions.

And those who are close to me betray me.

These are the times Jesus warned me of (St. Luke Chapter 21).

Then, why do I cry?

Jesus told me that I should pray, that if at all possible, I may escape these horrors!

Praise God! The Victims of the terrorist attack on America escaped!

There are no more tears, no more pain, suffering or horrors for them.

So why do I cry?

I cry tears of joy, I cry tears of joy because they escaped the hour of horrors, yet to come!

This is why I cry!

AFFORD

The Joy of Suffering

You are probably saying to yourself, what in the world is Audrey talking about. There is no joy in pain! And everyone knows that pain is pain! There is nothing Audrey can tell me to convince me that there is joy in pain and suffering.

Oh, yes I can. Let me tell you when it comes to suffering and pain, there was nothing that anyone could tell me to convince me that there was joy in suffering either. People use to tell me the pain of giving birth to a baby was joy! They were not about to fool me with that lie. In fact, I had been totally convinced that because I had cesarean delivery with my three children, I was born to be free of pain and suffering. I was put to sleep and I did not have to push!

Well, I am not talking about physical pain, such as having babies, cuts, scratches, bruises, burns or broken body parts. I am talking about the pain of a broken heart, the pain of sin, the pain of wanting to do right, but always end up doing wrong. I am talking about Spiritual Pain and Suffering!

Many of us suffer spiritual pain, because our lives moment by moment hang in the balance of good and evil. We are living in a world that is involved in spiritual warfare everyday. And believe it or not, many of us do not even realize that we are at war with the spirits of the world (which are Satan demons) and the spirit of Heaven the Holy Spirit of God!

The reason that many of us suffer is so wonderful. We suffer because we are the children of God. And for this reason we live our lives in spiritual warfare. It is the Holy Spirit of God that lives in us that is fighting sin and the evil spirits of the world.

All of us have desire truth! It is written in Psalms 51:6 that "Behold, You desire truth in the inward parts and in the hidden part you will make me to know wisdom." And it is true, but we have conformed to the ways of the world and we do not live according to the principles of God! We have not forgotten about God and unfortunately fell victims to the lies and deceit of Satan. We find joy in the world doing the things that seems to bring to us fun and no problems or commitments. And yes, nine times out of ten, these things are sinful and against the principles of God.

The things of the world brings temporary joy. There are many of us who are self-centered and seekers of our own joy and peace. And we always end up suffering. We have forgotten who and what God is! We forgot what God has done for us. We forgot that it is Gods will for us that will be done, even if it is suffering! Is it not Gods will that gave us life and that gives us everlasting life? Who else can do for you what God can do? News Flash! NO ONE!

Okay, so where does the joy of suffering come in? The Joy of suffering comes because we are heirs of Jesus Christ! One day I was at the bus stop talking to an elderly woman, complaining about my pain and suffering. I was telling her that I was so tired of the Devil bothering me. The woman said to me, "Child, Thank God that the Devil is still bothering you, because if he wasn't, that means that he has got you!" And she went on to say to me, "be glad that the Devil is bothering you," because it meant that I belong to Jesus! She said the Devil don't bother his own!

This elderly woman had given me a revelation! Right then and there I knew that I would rather suffer and try to be Christ like than to lose my soul to Satan! I am not going to tell you that I enjoy suffering. What I am telling you is that I have more joy and peace in my life knowing that my suffering is for my life with Jesus and the kingdom of heaven.

It is written in Romans 8:17 that, "If, then, we are children, we are also heirs; heirs indeed of God, and joint heirs with Christ Jesus, provided we suffer together that we may also be glorified together." Well I am blessed. I have not been beaten, spat upon, crucified or nailed to a cross with nails in my hands and feet, with a reef of thorns for a crown stuck on my head! No! I do not enjoy suffering, but it is the reason that I suffer that gives me joy! And it is because "To (me) the privilege was given in behalf of Christ, not only to put (my) faith in Him, but also to suffer in His behalf." Philippians 1:29.

Jesus gives me the strength to endure whatever suffering I might encounter as I do His will and live according to His principles. I don't mind because it is written in 1 Peter 4:1 that, "Therefore since Christ suffered in the flesh, too arm (myself) with the same mental disposition; because the person that has suffered in the flesh has desisted from sins!" Knowing this again I say, yes, it gives to me much joy. It gives me joy to suffer knowing that in 1 Peter 1:11 that "after (I) have suffered a little while, the God of all undeserved kindness, who called (me) to His everlasting glory in union with Christ, will Himself finish (my) training, He will make (me) firm, He will make (me) strong." Guess What? He will do it for you too!

Trust in God and do good. Resist temptation to do evil. Always pray, asking God for His protection and help. God knows that we are in spiritual warfare and that we are suffering. The joy of suffering is that we are joint heirs with Christ Jesus!

Audrey F. Evans-Ford

A *ngry for not listening to*
G *od, knowing that it was*
O *ur Savior Jesus that took*
N *ails in His hands for*
Y *es, Our Salvation!*

The Times I forgot About Jesus

It shames me to tell you this, but I must! There were so many times that I fell into sin. There is no greater pain, than the pain of disobeying the laws of God. Your heart hurts, it beats at a wild and rapid paste, sometimes making your chest hurt. The tightness in your chest is so bad that you have to rub it! You think maybe you are about to have a heart attack! You become light headed and dizzy. Your body begins to feel like putty and you feel as though you are about to collapse! You say to yourself, "I give up, just let me die!"

You don't. You just keep on praying and hoping that God will quickly take away the pain. Still, the pain is there and it seems as though you will have this pain for the rest of your life. You feel as though you have committed the last, the greatest, the ultimate sin. Whatever that might be. And this time the pain and torment is forever. You begin to believe that God will not forgive you this time. Guess what? He will! He will forgive you and comfort you. He will rescue you and bless you. And the greatest thing about it all is that, when he heals you taking away your hurt and pain, you won't remember any of it! It is as though, the pain and hurt was never there.

The sad thing about this wonderful healing is; "Once we have been forgiven and healed, we do it again. We forget about Jesus!" We forget about the pain and suffering we went through. Like a mother giving birth, she has such excruciating labor pain. She just can't bare the pain anymore. She screams and hollers. She wants to die. She can't take the pain anymore! Then once the child has been birth, it brings to her so much joy, she do not remember the pain.

Yeah, when we forget our pain we forget about Jesus! And fall right back into Satan trap! It is written in Deuteromy 4:31 "So they refused to listen and they did not remember your wonderful acts that you performed with them." When we are suffering, we call Jesus begging Him for mercy. Making promises that we will do this or that whatever it takes, Lord Jesus, please take away this pain! Jesus I am so sorry please forgive me!

It does not matter how many times we sin offending our Lord, He still gives to us His mercy, forgiving us for our unrighteous deeds and never reminding us of them. Does this mean that we are suppose to forget that Jesus forgave us, took away our pain, restored our life, giving to us another chance? Or do we have to suffer again and again and again to remember Jesus? I did!

Jesus is so merciful and full of grace! He always answers our prayers, healing us and saving us. And after the pain and suffering is gone, the memory is gone. The memory of what Jesus has done for us! I am guilty of this and I ask my Lord and Savior right now for forgiveness. "Lord Jesus please forgive me for the times I forgot about you!"

Thank you Jesus for forgiving me and giving me back my life. Thank you for healing me! Thank you Jesus for your loving kindness and faithfulness. Thank you for not forgetting me!

**Note, "Satan gave us that pain and Jesus took it away! Remember Satan is the cause of the pain in our lives.

"Don't Forget About Jesus after the pain is gone!"

Acknowledge, Beware and Recognize

I Will Remember

I will remember to keep God first in my life. Thanking Him for His love, grace, mercy and forgiveness.

I will remember to think before I speak. Speaking words that are beneficial to the spiritual progress of others.

I will remember that whatever I do or say, that God is watching me and He hears me!

I will remember by the grace of God to continually rid myself of all filth and evilness.

I will remember to always keep my faith in Jesus Christ, trusting my life only unto Him.

I will remember to be humble and accept the word of God that is planted in my heart.

I will remember that fun in the "WORLD" results in "SIN!"

I will remember that fun in the "WORD" results in joy, peace and eternal happiness!

I will remember to continually Praise and Worship God, thanking Him for His many blessing!

I will remember that not only did Christ live for me, but that He also suffered and died for me!

I will remember to "REMEMBER" that it is God that gave me life!

Audrey F. Evans-Ford

The Principle of Life

My son and I were talking one night about God and our savior Jesus Christ. Troy mentioned that he did not understand why we have to go through Jesus for our Father God to receive our prayers. Why can't we pray directly to God after all He is our Father. My son knows Jesus and he loves Jesus. But, he was confused because he said that he felt that he was dishonoring God and not placing Him on high where He is, by praying to Jesus instead of Him.

For some reason at that moment I could not find the words to explain to Troy why we must go to Jesus for Our Father to receive our prayers. I told Troy at that time not to dwell on it and do not confuse him self about it. But as he becomes intimate with Jesus all of his questions will be answered. The Spirit of God will give him the wisdom and knowledge that he seeks. And this is written in the book of Hebrew 10:15-16 that the "Holy Spirit also witness to us. This is the covenant that I (The Lord God) will make with them. I will put my laws into your heart and in your minds I will write them." I also told him that God was listening to him and understands what he is dealing with. God will guide him and answer him.

Troy and I talked very briefly about the time that I felt that way. Thank God for not holding us accountable for the things that we have said and done out of ignorance. I Praise God for His love and understanding! I mentioned the time that I said that I loved my son Troy, more than I loved Jesus! Yes, I said this thing and at the time I meant it with all my heart. I did not know then what I know now.

You see, I had prayed for a son and God answered my prayer and gave to me a wonderful son. So I thought that I was suppose to love my son more than Gods Son because God loved His son more than He loved mine. I thought I was to love my son the same way! Anyway, it was ignorance on my part, just plain old ignorant!

I did not know that God loves all of us just as much as He loves His son Jesus Christ. And there is no way that any one can say that this is not true. God sent His only begotten son into this cure world of sin to live as one of us, to suffer, to be crucified and die for us!

Anyway it bothered me that I did not have an answer for Troy that night. I went to sleep with this on my mind. I really could not sleep. So, I did what I always do when I can't sleep, I talked to Jesus! I talked to Jesus about how it baffled me that I actually did not have an answer for Troy. Praise the Lord! So, the Holy Spirit told to me what to do. He told me to write this story and give it to Troy. He gave me the wisdom and the knowledge to write this, giving Troy the answer that he was seeking.

Why do we have to go through Jesus for God our Father to receive our prayers? Because it is the "Principle of Life." Think about it, we always have to go through something to get somewhere. We always have to go through someone to get to someone else. For Examples: The President. Can you go directly to the President with your request? I think not! Businesses. Can you go directly to the Owner of a large corporation and ask for a job? Nope! But if you knew them personally and were sitting right beside them, you could.

Our Father has given Jesus "All Authority" over the heavens and the earth. Our Father does not even Judge us. He has committed all the judging to His Son Jesus Christ. God did this in order that we all may honor His Son just as we honor Him. And whoever does not honor His Son Jesus does not honor Him, our Father who sent Him. This is written in John 5:22-23.

It is written in Philippians 2:9-11 that God our Father has exalted His Son Jesus Christ to a superior position and kindly gave Him the name that is above every name. It is for this very reason that every knee in heaven and on earth and under the ground should bend in the name of Jesus. And every tongue should openly acknowledge that Jesus Christ is Lord to the glory of God the Father!

This is the "Principle of Life" you have to go through someone to reach the one at the top! This is the same principle with God and His Son Jesus Christ who is seated at His right hand. You are not seated at the right hand of our Father! Jesus is the Son of God. He is our Savior and our Intercessor. This is why you and I must go to Jesus and ask Him to receive our prayers.

Jesus will take our prayer to our Father and our Father will receive and answer them!

"This is the will of God in union with his Son Jesus Christ!"
(Thessalonians 5:17)

Audrey F. Evans-Ford

RECOGNIZE SATAN'S WORK"

Obedient to The Right Voice

In 1999 because of a very troubled marriage involving drugs, alcohol, fighting and always being torn apart from my husband, I knew that I needed help and I called Jesus! My husband and I both know Jesus and we knew Him then. Our troubled marriage was because we did not living according to the laws and principles of God and we did not let Jesus in our lives. We let our lives be controlled by man and the ways of the world.

March of 1999 a voice kept speaking to me, telling me to write. So, I began to write. I began writing a book about my personal opinions about how we should live our lives and give them to Christ. My husband and I were separated at that particular time. Anyway, after I had begun writing the book again, my husband and I got back together. I am telling you all of this for you to understand what I am about to tell you about being obedient to the right voice!

The voice that announced to me to write this book told me at that particular time, not to resume living with my husband. The voice also told me why. But there was also another voice speaking to me. It was the voice of the liar, our adversary, the Devil. It was the voice that causes us to doubt and not trust God. It was the voice of the adversary telling me, "You better get your husband back before another woman gets him!" But the voice of the righteous one kept telling me not to do it at that time. He would tell me when. The voice told me why. The righteous voice also told me that He knew that I did not trust Him and I had no faith! I said that I did, but I did'nt! I did not have faith nor did I trust God with my marriage and I resumed it!

The voice that I did not have faith and trust in, told me what would happen and it did. I was told that my marriage would not last and that we would go through the same thing again and again and we did. In fact we are separated now. The voice explained to me in detail that I would not complete the book at that time if I had resumed living

Acknowledge, Beware and Recognize

with my husband and I did'nt. The voice also explained that I was putting my lust for the flesh before God!

Boy was I dense. I put my husband before God and I ignored Gods call and I was disobedient to the voice of the Holy Spirit. I listened to the voice of the Devil. That is the biggest mistake anyone could ever make, listening to the wrong voice, the Devil's voice. And guess what? I knew the difference in the voices and yet I listened to the wrong voice. Because, I did not have faith or trust in God!

Jesus told me not to worry about my marriage because it was not dead, but that I had to do what God had called me to do first. Jesus was telling me all along that I could not do what God had called me to do at that time and be in a relationship with my husband. Jesus told me that I had to first get my life right with God. He said that He would strengthen me and that I would be a blessing to many people. Jesus knows all there is to know about me and He knew that I could not do both at the same time, be in an unsaved marriage and do what God called me to do! Jesus knew that I would fall again!

I am telling you that listening to the wrong voice will cause you nothing but pain, heartache, tumbling and falling. I know, been there, done that! But, let me tell you this! "ANYTHING" that the Devil makes bad, God always makes it "Better!" Praise the Lord! Oh, the voice of lies and deceit are not going to stop just because you give your life to Christ. In fact, they will speak to you even more.

I thank God for discernment. I know the difference in the voices. And now I have learned to be obedient to the right voice. Satan tried to stop me from doing what God had called me to do. I admit listening to Satan caused a slight delay! Or did he? You know man seem to have forgotten that God is in control of all that exists! God is in control of every life, situation and circumstance!

I assure you, that whatever Satan makes bad God makes it better. Believe it! God does make it "Better!" Here is an example of God making things better; "If I would have completed this book not knowing what I know today, this book would have been prematurely written and not the work of God." It would have been the work of Satan. Let me explain to you why. The original title for this book was: "Hey It's Just My Opinion." An author whom I had asked for help in getting this book published, responded to my request for his help. In his response he stated that he found my writing to be very interesting and thought provoking. I took this as a compliment and I was thrilled. I have potential! I am going to be a writer!

Like I said, I was thrilled. But the voice spoke to me again, in His sweet, calm and loving tone and simply said to me, "Audrey is it potential or is this a gift that God has given to you?" Then I said to myself, "Okay, Audrey you know the answer!" And I did and I do! This writing that I do is not potential, it is a gift from God! I realized that I have to stay on guard and watch out for that Liar, Satan! Satan had slivered his way into my thoughts and writing and I was about to write things that would provoke readers and upset them causing anger. This was not the will of God!

The voice that I have been telling you about is the voice of the Holy Spirit! The Holy Spirit is Gods Spirit manifested in me. He speaks, announces and declares to me the things that are to come and the things that God wants me to do! The Spirit announced to me to change the title of this book and to edit all the stories. He explained to me that the title "Hey It's Just My Opinion" is itself provoking. It would surely catch the eyes of many readers. And most likely many would purchase the book with an attitude ready to rebel, attacking the author on anything that was not their opinion! This means that the book would cause some sort of controversy! This is not what God called me to do. Opinions are tools of the Devil. The Devil causes us to use the tool of opinions for the soul purpose of causing conflict among one another causing us to fight with each other!

I was not assigned to write a book to provoke or upset anyone. I was appointed to write this book to help the lost to find God. God wants His children to acknowledge Satan, to be ware of Satan and to recognize Satan's work. God wants us to have discernment and be obedient to the right voice!

I did like Eve. I disobeyed God! Eve knew the voice of God. She knew what God had told her to do and not to do! Instead of listening and being obedient to the voice of God, Eve listened to the Devil. God told Eve not to eat of the forbidden fruit or she would surely die. Then as it is written in Genesis 3:4, Satan, the Devil himself comes along and says to Eve, "eat of the forbidden fruit, you positively will not die!" Satan lied! What happened to Eve? She died! Thank God for His grace and mercy or I surely would have died too!

Pray for discernment of the voices. Don't let the Devil deceive you anymore. Be obedient to God! "**Be obedient to the Right Voice!**"

"And Always Stay On Guard With God!"

Audrey F. Evans-Ford

Obeying The Ministry

I was raised up as an Episcopalian. Growing up in an Episcopal Church, I did not believe in other religions or any other ways to serve God. The Episcopal way was the only way! Thank God for blessing those who honestly just do not know! A Christian is a person who believes in Christ and we all serve the same, one and only God! Our Father in Heaven and His Son Christ Jesus!

There was a time that I thought television ministries were all fake ministers. I thought it was all a con to take old peoples money. I remember back in the days when Reverend Ike was ministering on TV. In fact, whatever happened to him? Anyway, I remember so many elderly people that seemed to live more by faith in him than they did in God. Well I was young then and I truly did not know much about religion or different ministries.

Oh and the thought of going to a Baptist Church was simply absurd! I had heard so many rumors about Baptist Preachers being backsliders and messing with the women in the churches. It was just no way in the world that I would even think of letting them preach the word of God to me! Then there was the rumor that they took the money from the church to buy themselves a new "Caddy." No, there was no way I was going to attend that type of church! Thank God, I know now that this is the work of the Devil. And personally, no I do not know of any Ministers that have taken Church finances and used them for personal gain.

I realize that Religion and Christianity are two different things. Christianity is living a Christ like life, being like Jesus. Religion is how we choose to serve and worship God. And you need to know that "Not all people who proclaims religion are godly." This is why Jesus tells us in Matthew 7:15 to; "Beware of false prophets, who come to you in sheep's clothing, but inwardly they are raven wolves." Jesus says that we will know them by their fruit. Jesus also tells us in Matthew 13:17 to "Obey those who rule over you (us) and be submissive for they watch out for your (our) souls, as those who must give account. Let them do so with joy and not with grief for that would be unprofitable for you (us). And Jesus says in Matthew 23:3,

Acknowledge, Beware and Recognize

"Therefore, whatever they tell you (us) to observe, that observe and do, but do not do according to their works, for they say and do not do." In other words, they (ministers) do not practice what they preach! Ministers, Priest, Pastors, Preachers or whatever title that they chose to use, they are ministers of religious laws and they are official interpreters of the Holy Scriptures!

It is also written in 1 Peter 4:10-11 that "If anyone speaks, let him speak as the oracles of God. (This includes you too!) If anyone ministers, let him do it as with the ability which God supplies, that in all things God may be glorified through Jesus Christ, to whom belong the glory and the dominion forever and ever Amen!"

Obeying and respecting the ministry is honoring God. We must remember to obey the laws and principles of our Father. We must practice and obey our ministry and be careful not to follow the example of wolves in sheep clothes. I understand exactly what Jesus means by this. Like myself, I personally know a few ministers that minister the word of God with such an impact that they make you tremble inside, chills run through your body, you want to jump up and down and just shout Thank you God! And after they have ministered the word of God, their hearts are numb! The love of God that they preached, you do not see in them.

But, it is okay because God loves them too and they are doing what God has called and anointed them to do. They are ministering Gods word to us! This is their calling and we must not turn on them nor judge them! If we turn on our ministry or judge our ministry, then we dishonor God!

This is what Satan wants us to do! Don't Do It! Don't let Satan pull you away from the Church or the Ministry. This is another one of Satans' attacks on Gods children. He wants the children of God to become angry with the Ministers. Satan wants us to judge them and put them down. Satan wants us to turn away from all of our Churches. Again, I say to you, "Don't Do It!"

Instead, Pray for our Ministers they are like us, they are human too! Ministers are children of God called to lead us! They are not above reproach from Satan attacks no more than you or I. They need our prayers just as we need theirs. Don't judge them, love them and respect them. God does!

Acknowledge, Recognize and Beware! SATAN "Ain"t no joke! He is coming after Gods children with a vengeance!

Audrey F. Evans-Ford

S *truggling*
T *rying to do right and*
R *esist the Devil, wanting to*
E *agerly serve God, and the enemy*
S *atan keeps on trying to*
S *teal our strength and wear us down!*

Then and Now

The day I decided to accept Christ in my life was the day I began to seek all knowledge of Him. I began looking everywhere and asking everyone that I knew were Christians, questions about Jesus and the Bible. One day it just hit me, I remembered that Jesus said, "For every one that ask receives; and he that seek find; and to him that knock, the door will be opened." This is written in the book of Luke 11:10. I was seeking knowledge and I received it! Thank You Jesus for your Spirit that speaks to me!

I began to remember how I reacted to other people talking about they received the Holy Ghost! *Note, I said Holy Ghost, this is what the Holy Spirit is also called. It is a personal thing with me, I much rather call our Comforter and Helper, which is of God, The Holy Spirit. I just can't conceive The Spirit of God as a Ghost, because the Spirit is alive, not dead. Anyway I remembered when I was a little girl. My Mom took my sister and I to a small Baptist Church in the country. Well being an Episcopalian and never having been in another Church other than our Family Church my sister and I did not understand what was happening.

First of all we were little girls, we were about nine and ten years old at the time. Of course, I am the oldest. I remember it was Mothers Day and a neighbor had invited my Mom to her church. I remember the pretty white dresses that my sister and I wore with a red rose attached to the shoulder of our dresses. When we arrived at the church, the first thing that I noticed was the cemetery right beside the church. I was not happy about that. Here we are in the country at a little white wooden Church, lawn of red dirt and a cemetery right beside it! I was not thrilled at all!

We entered the Church and its congregation was full. There was a whole lot of shouting, singing, praising the Lord and Preaching going on. This scene was foreign to my sister and I. There was this one particular woman that stood up. She was a very heavy woman. She began to jump up and down, and the church was shaking, she was screaming and shouting, I think she was crying too! All of a sudden she hit the floor. It seemed as though the whole church was going to collapse. This frightened my sister and I. We thought that the woman had died and we jumped up and ran out of the Church. We were afraid because we did not know what was happening, this was new to us. Anyway, that was "Then."

Today, almost four decades later, I know now what happened that day back "THEN!" I know about the Holy Spirit, and who He is! Jesus tells us in John 14:17-18 and 26 that, "The Spirit of truth; know Him and He dwells with you and He shall be in you! I will come to you." This means that those of us who live in the word and are obedient to the word of God, that the Holy Spirit will come upon you (and alive in you)! The Comforter, which is the Holy Spirit will teach you (us) all things and bring all things to your remembrance, whatsoever Jesus have!" Praise the Lord!

I asked Jesus to change me, making me whatever it is that He wants me to be. I asked Jesus to renew my mind and make my thoughts agreeable to His will. I asked Jesus to cleanse my heart and renew my spirit. He did it! I accept Jesus as Lord over my life. Jesus has healed me and cleansed me of all my unrighteous deeds. And He has filled me with His Holy Spirit! How do I know that the Holy Spirit is in me? I know because, "The Fruit of the Spirit is love, joy, peace, long-suffering, gentleness, goodness, faith, meekness, temperance, and against such there is no law!" I have it all!

I know that I am filled with the Holy Spirit because the Bible says in Galatians 5:22-25 "They that belong to Christ have crucified the flesh with the affections and lust." My flesh has been crucified because Jesus redeemed me, making me the righteousness of God our Father through His shed blood and every evil work of the adversary within me is destroyed!

"**NOW**" I know the Holy Spirit and what He does. He lives in me. No, I do not jump up and down, or faint. When I hear Him speak to me, I just smile and say, "Thank You Jesus! There are times that I feel the Holy Spirit presence flowing, surging through my body like a current of electrical energy causing me to tremble inside. I feel like I am levitated, floating on a cloud. I love those moments because it is He the Spirit of God that confirms that He lives in me and is effectually at work in me. And He is "**AWESOME!**"

I have learned that it does not matter what religious denomination that you are, the Holy Spirit is the same for us all. The Holy Spirit is of God and is God! And it is written in Luke 12:12 that "The Holy

Acknowledge, Beware and Recognize

Spirit teaches you (all of us) in the same hour what you (we) ought to say!" The Holy Spirit announces and declares the things to us that our Father would have us to do. Know that being the righteousness of our Father God that you are heir to all that belongs to Him. Yes even His Spirit, who lives in you too!

Nope! I did not know that "**THEN**" but I know it "**NOW**" not what the Holy Spirit is, but "WHO" He is! He is the Spirit of God!

Audrey F. Evans-Ford

Religion is Division

Yes, it is true that religion is division. It is the division of Gods people. This division causes Gods children to fight against one another. Each religious organization thinks that their religious way of serving God is better than the others. There is jealousy, envy, and less love for one another as brothers and sisters in Christ. The different religions have become competitive instead of godly and being one with Christ. Religion was not meant to separate Gods children it was meant to be a means of worshiping, serving and honoring God our Father showing Him our love for Him. Religion was meant to be a way to teach of Gods love, His laws and His principles. I know that there is someone reading this right now that knows what I am talking about.

I have for this reason denounced religion. No, I am not telling you that I no longer go to Church or Bible studies and other Christian (religious) gatherings. I will never stop seeking knowledge about Jesus Christ and a way to better serve Him. It is my greatest desirer to be closer to Jesus. Oh, and I am determined to live my life according to Gods laws and principles. I am a Christian and yes, I do believe in Jesus Christ! I know Jesus He is my Savior!

When I looked at my religious background, I began to reminisce about what church was like for me coming up. I remember the color barrier in the Church among the Church members, right there in Gods Temple! We are here in Gods' temple worshipping Him, praising Him and giving Him the glory and yet we have a racial issue right in the church. Yes, it is true, we have color issues in the churches too! What part do we not understand? We are all Gods children and He loves us all! God loves all colors. Look at the rainbow!

Then Church service let out and many times, some one is barely out of the door and they are offended about something. Their nose is bent out of shape and in the air! This is not a Christian thing to do. Theses are two of the things that show division in the Church among its own members. Where is the love of Christ? To claim Christianity; you are claiming Christ in your life. And if you have claimed Christ,

Acknowledge, Beware and Recognize

then you have claim a mind and a heart like Christ! Therefore, as a Christian, you are to be like Christ.

Let me talk about the division in religion. You see, each religious organization feels that their way of serving God is the best way. This causes a little and sometimes a lot of animosity among the Churches. I remember when I was growing up, that the Baptist did not agree with the Catholics and the Catholics sure did not agree with the Baptist. It is still like this today! And it is causing the separation of Gods children. I am not writing about this to offend or to bring disgrace to the Churches. So, please before you burn this book, hear me out!

I used the Baptist and the Catholic Churches as an example to show you the division that religion cause. There are many different type of religions, Holiness, Pentacostal, Methodist, Jehovah Witnesses, Episcopal, Islamic, Lutheran, and many more. They all acknowledge Christ and live to serve God giving their love and devotion. All these religious organizations are serving God in the way that they feel is most righteous. This is a good thing, because no matter what your religion is we are all loving and serving God!

The division in religion did not just happen. God even speaks of the division of men in Exodus 19:6 "And you yourselves will become to me a kingdom of priests and a holy nation." This statement tells you (when it says, priests) that there is more than one religion because they are from different nations. But, they will all come to God and be "ONE" Holy Nation!

Have you figured out what I am trying to tell you? I am telling you that the author of confusion has done his job. This is the work of Satan. He is busy trying to separate and destroy Gods' children. Remember his work in the Garden of Eden? Satan did not stop there!

Satan is determined to steal Gods children! He knows why God sent His Son Jesus Christ into the world. Yes, Jesus came that we might live in the kingdom of heaven! Satan began deceiving man in the Garden of Eden. Satan knows that the children of God are weak, so he has been having a ball deceiving us. And the thing about it is that he has been and still is so good at it!

Satan tactics are so obvious, he attacks us individually, one on one. Yeah, he is pretty smart. He knows the principle of "United we stand, Divided we fall" This is why we should be wiser! Sure there is division in the Churches because of religion. But, if we as individuals, call upon Jesus Christ and establish a personal and intimate relationship with Him, we can defeat Satan!

We should also establish a personal relationship with Jesus because Jesus tells us in Matthew 11:27 that "All things have been delivered to me (Him) by my (His) Father, and no one fully knows the Son (Him) but the Father, neither does anyone fully know the Father but the Son and anyone to whom the Son is willing to reveal Him." Is not this a good enough reason for you to have a personal relationship with Jesus?

When you and I become intimate with Jesus, the closer we become to God and to one another. And when we become closer to Jesus we become closer to one another and united, no longer divided! Then Satan is defeated! Praise God and Thank Jesus!

My religion "Today" is this:

R esisting Satan! No longer being blind to his

E vilness, tricks, deceit and

L ies, nor blind by his

I llusions but, to be drawn closer

G etting very

I ntimate with God

O ur Father and Jesus Christ our savior, living for the

N ew Kingdom – **Heaven!**

I am one with Christ Jesus, and it is He (Jesus) that is within me that is greater than he (Satan) that is in this world. I am united in Christ where there is no "Division"! Come on be united in Christ!

Eve and Adam

In the beginning there was Adam and Eve. Today we have "Eve and Adam." This came about the day that Eve bit the forbidden fruit. In Genesis 3:3-4 Adam and Eve were told, "But of the fruit of the tree which is in the midst of the garden, God hath said, 'Ye shall not eat of it, neither shall ye touch it, lest ye die." And the serpent said unto the woman, ye shall not surely die." We have heard the story about how Eve disobeyed God, bit the forbidden fruit and shared it with Adam.

This was the beginning of women dominating men. And this happened thousands and thousands of years before women started fighting for equal rights. I call the women of today, the daughters of Eve. They fought for equal rights, the right to be treated like men. According to the law of man, women are now equal to man. Back in the seventies, there was a television commercial, about cigarettes saying, "You've Come A Long Way Baby?" Well the commercial was right. Women have come a long way and (farther in sin.) Many women seem to have forgotten Gods law and the reason for their existence. Of, course this is Satan's work! Who did he deceive in the Garden? Okay.

It is written in Genesis 2:18 that God said, "It is not good that man should be alone; I will make him a helper comparable to him." So, God made woman to be a mate for man not to be equal to man. Woman was not made to dominate man or to rule man! *Note, God created man in His image, "Adam" and God "made" woman "Eve" from the rib of man. And Adam named her like he named everything else in the Garden, and he called her woman because she was bone of his bones and flesh of his flesh, taken from his rib.

The daughters of Eve today are dominating men in their personal lives and on jobs. Some women actually take the man's physical role. There was a song in the mid-sixties with the lyrics: "Girls You Can't Do Like The Guys You Know And Still Be A Lady." Ahhhh, Excuse Me! Are you talking to me?

Some women think that they can be both, a man and a woman. That they can do the job of a man, then come home, take a bubble bath and still be a lady. On the other hand what about the man that plays the reverse role? He is home all day with the children. He does the cooking and the cleaning. So, how do we treat the HOUSEband, like a lady or a man?

What happened to the love, honor and respect the man? There are so many women wanting and waiting to take their jobs and their roles in life. What do these women want the men to do? Become extinct?

Here is an example of what I am talking about in reference to the Eves' of today. Millie Huges-Ford is a professor at the University of California and an osteoporosis researcher. Ms. Ford has flown on the space shuttle in 1991 and she knows that weightlessness cause bone loss in both sexes. Ms. Ford is especially interested in whether women loose bone and calcium at the same rate in space as men. But she wants an all female crew to go into space.

The thing that baffles me is this, why would Ms. Ford want an all female crew to find out the rate of bone and calcium lose in both the sexes, but want an all female crew. Why not have both, a male and female crew? Would it not be more logical to have both sexes on this flight to find out the rate in which both sexes lose bone and calcium in space?

Another Eve of today, Ms Nancy Mace, the first woman to graduate form the Charleston Citadel. I agree with Ms. Virginia Geraty who is an older Charlestonian affiliated with the college. She had been associated with The Citadel men as a lecturer. Ms. Geraty said, "The mighty fortress has fallen and striped of its tradition and manly character, by a woman." And she is right! Ms Geraty also says that "The farewell service should be held for The Citadel with a twenty one gun salute, taps and lowering the flag as the old soldier fades away." Girls enjoy your victory!

I understand a female being intrigued by the Military Uniforms and even the military life style. I love the Military Uniforms myself. There is so much honor, dignity and respect that the uniform portrays and carries. But, why in the world would females want to intrude on the male society and their privacy? Why are females forcing themselves into all male institutions? The answer is really simple. These women are the Eves of today and they are not listening to God!

It is amazing, that when Eve was made that she was given the name "Eve" only to be persuaded by the "Evil" one and disobey Gods first commandment. Eve committed the first sin in the world! She disobeyed God and listened to the voice of Satan! Many women today still disobey God and listen to the voice of Satan! Ladies beware and recognize the work of Satan!

No, I am not telling you to stay barefoot, pregnant and in the kitchen. I am telling you to "Stay on Guard with God"

Audrey F. Evans-Ford

The Commandment of Marriage

I do not know the divorce rate of today. I have never taken an interest in divorce rates and I am still not interested. Divorce and separation is a broken commandment of God! God has not changed His commandment. God's word stand firm in Heaven and His word extends to every generation, including this one! And No! Divorce neither separation is acceptable to God. It is still a sin! Who is man to change the commandment of God? Satan has deceived us. Believing that it is okay to separate and divorce, man still continues to ignore God's commandment.

It is written in the book of Matthew 19:3-6 that when the Pharisees tested Jesus asking Him, "Is it lawful for a man to divorce his wife for just any reason?" Jesus answered and said to them, "Have you not read that He who made them at the beginning made them male and female, and said, "For this reason a man shall leave his father and mother and be joined to his wife, and the two shall become one flesh? Therefore, what God has joined together, let not man separate!" Moses was a man. He was not and is not God! Moses cannot change the law of God, but because of the hardheartedness of man, he permitted the concession of divorce. But, this is not Gods will from the beginning. And it is not Gods will to the end! God said that what He Has yoked together let no man put apart! Not even Moses!

Many marriages end in separation and divorce because they are made in the world with worldly desires and not in the word with a desire for life with Christ! Most people before they get married plan for their future, choosing the right mate. Choosing the one who will provide them with a home, car, children and mainly financial security! Their goal in life is material goal. The material of the world is their desire. Where is the love or shall I say what kind of love is this? I assure you that marrying for financial security, that the love vows that you take last as long as the finance. When the finances are gone, so will the marriage, in many cases.

Then there are many divorces and separations because of adultery.

The reason is like I said, because most marriages were made in the world, not the word. Husbands and wives alike fornicate. They do not realize that (if believers) in Jesus Christ that their bodies are temples where the Holy Spirit to abides. They should avoid as written in 1 Corinthians 6:18 "Flee from fornication!" When you married you became one flesh and if you believe in Jesus Christ, then you need to know that your body is a member of His body. Your body is His temple. Think about it, would you take Jesus to lay with whores? Would you take our pure, sinless and Holy Lord to sin against His Father who is our Father too? Would you? Do you think that Jesus would even do such a thing? I say not! By all means we should glorify God in our bodies as well as in our hearts!

What happened to "Real Love?" The love that when two people marry saying to one another for better or for worst, for richer or poorer, in sickness and in health, until "Death do we part," loving each other whole-heartedly with tears of joy in your eyes! The vows you made in the presence of God! (Not necessarily in a Church) God is everywhere, all the time!

Love is patient and kind. Love is not jealous or boastful or proud or rude. Love does not demand its own way. Love is not irritable, and *"LOVES DOES NOT KEEP RECORD OF WHEN IT HAS BEEN WRONGED!"* **LOVE NEVER GIVES UP!** Love never loses faith, love is always hopeful and endures through every circumstance. Love last forever. There are three things that will endure, and it is written in 1 Corinthians chapter 13 and that is Faith, Hope and Love – and the greatest of these is LOVE!

Love is strong. Love is a lot stronger than most of us can comprehend or realize. Many of us because of the trials and tribulations in our marriages, we get tired and even confused. Let me tell you something. Anytime there is confusion in your marriage, you better believe, it did not just happen. It is the work of Satan. He enters into your marriage in many ways. He enters through family members, friends, finances, children, associates, strangers, drugs, alcohol, etc… Satan attacks that mind of yours. He gets to working on your nerves about this and that, whatever. Then there comes the stress of finances, stress from work, the children running you crazy, these are just some examples of Satan's work. He is putting pressure on you! He has worked you over to the point that you are ready to throw in the towel. You need to know that no matter what the problem is, that the problem is not what it is, but who it is! The problem is Satan! Yap! The Devil Himself!

D estroying
E ach and every
V ulnerable person who
I s not walking and
L iving in the word of God!

Satan is so good at what he does that he even has Ministers of the word preaching separation in the congregation! Tell me Satan is not busy! It is time that Gods' Children wake up and resist the evils of Satan and stop him from destroying our families!

In case you don't know it, Satan enjoys destroying our lives and families. Satan wants to destroy every single marriage that he can. And it is sad to say it, but he is successfully doing it by the millions. Satan's time is running out just like ours. And he is in a hurry to gather as many souls as he can, so he is doing it by the dozens. When Satan separates husbands and wives, he brings separation of children and other family members as well, and separates many from Christ! He knows that if he takes your joy he takes you from the Lord (even if it is only temporarily). Yes, only temporarily. You see the moment your joy is taken all you can think about is your pain and suffering for the moment. But, after that moment, what do you do? You begin remembering God and calling on Him to help you and to save you!

I know, been there, done that! Doing it now, calling on God asking Him everyday for mercy and forgiveness. Asking God to please continue to lead me in His path of righteousness. Praying that I will be strengthen to do His will and obey His commandment and live according to His principles. Praying that He will restore my marriage.

My husband and I are separated. Why? Because of my sins, backsliding and being weak temptation and sin! Satan has once again accomplished what he wanted. He has separated my husband and I. And he is still working on keeping us separated. I messed up! But, I have not given up and I will not give up! I have made many mistakes in my life, living in the world in sin. Guess what, I am tired of the same old troubles over and over again. I have given my life to Christ. I decided to live my life the way that Jesus would have me to live it. I will, I am determined to obedient to the laws of God and live according to His principle at whatever cost!

Satan knew my weakness and he attacked it! My marriage has been torn a part many times because of drugs and not enough love. I love my husband and I believe and I know in my heart that he in his own way love me too. After I had gotten baptized, my husband was so happy. He had even tried to come out of the world and into the word himself. But, I backslide indulging in drugs again. I remember one day my husband asked me, what was he doing wrong now to make me do drugs. I answered him honestly telling him that it was not anything that he had done or was doing. Deep inside I knew it was Satan, but I knew that my husband, (like many peoples) did not want to hear nothing about the Devil! Well, Satan did have his part in it. But, I can't blame him, it was my own weakness, I fell. And once I began to slide I just could not get my grip. Anyway, my husband finally could not take anymore of me and the drugs and the things that I was doing, like taking his money! He threw me out of his Dads house and into the streets. And I threw him back into the world with Satan! He got caught in the Devil's snare.

I lost what little that I did have. I really did not have a place to stay. Well no place that I wanted to stay. I ended up living in a place where I was placed in the mist of the very thing that was the cause of my separation, "Drugs!" I fought the urge to use drugs again and I was unsuccessful. Then I realized all that had happened to me was the work of Satan in my life. He had to take my joy. He thought that taking my husband away from me would keep me from doing what God called me to do! He wanted to weaken me, make me give up and destroy me!

Wrong! Satan only made me stronger and more determine to do the will of my Father God. Through all my suffering and pain, I have been given peace and joy. Jesus kept His promise to me. He has shown me favor. He has given to me grace and shown me mercy. Sure, my husband and I are still separated. But, it is okay, because you see, Jesus assured me that I can pray and ask for anything in His name and will have it. This is written in Mark 11:22. Jesus cannot tell a lie. All that is required of me is that I believe and have no doubt in my heart. I know that my prayers have been answered. Jesus says in Luke11:9, to Keep asking, for whatever I ask, I will receive (my marriage restored) and that everyone (including me) who asks shall be given whatever they ask! This is the word of Jesus the Son of God, Our Father who has given Him (Jesus) all authority in the heaven and the earth. I kept asking and I still ask for my marriage to be restored and I know that it is done. I'm standing on Jesus word of promise to me! I am waiting for the manifestation! I know that Jesus is effectually at work answering my prayer.

You know sometimes we take a coffee break, just to relax for a minute or two. Guess What? Satan does not take a break, I know that he would not probably want to take a coffee break, but you would think maybe he would like to take an "Ice Water" break! But, no, he much rather bother us! I am telling you from my personal experience, he just won't let up! He is just terrible! But, our Father God is Awesome and Powerful! He will not let Satan have his way with us!

We must stop being deceived by Satan and his lies. For our sake we need to obey the commandments of God. We can stop the separation of our families by accepting Jesus Christ in our lives.

All things are possible through Jesus, He is the only one that can save us and give us salvation!

Man can rewrite the commandments all he want to, but man surely cannot change the word of God nor His laws and principles. Look, being heirs to Christ means that we are married to Him. Do you want to Divorce God? Well, when we break Gods commandments, it is the same as separating from Him and divorcing Him? Sin separates us from God! Think about it!

In 1 Corinthians 7:17 we are told that we must at whatever cost, accept whatever situation the Lord has put us in and continue on as we were when God first called us. So you see, for better or for worst you should stay married and trust God to fix whatever the problem is. This is if you have Christ in you life. Our Lord Jesus lived, suffered and died for us. What are we willing to do for Him?

Is Jesus not worth giving up the things of the world? Jesus is not asking us to sacrifice our lives. He is offering us a better life. Jesus has already made the sacrifice for us. He gave His life!

Remember Jesus suffered for you and I! He was beaten and lashed. He had to carry a cross, which only God knows how much it weighed, then He was nailed to it! Don't just imagine, try to feel

His pain as He hung on the cross! Jesus suffering for you and I, because of our sins and Satan lies and deceit!

To all of you who are married, rather separated or even divorced, think about what you are doing or what you have done. Remember God never and God never will instruct separation or divorce. It is a lie

Acknowledge, Beware and Recognize

of the Devil to get you to sin against our Father. To get you to break His commandment! Be aware of Satan, he is the god of the world and the serpent of deceit. And like the snake that he is, he slivers his way into our lives, destroying us with the poison of his world. Thank our Father for the **Antidote**, "**The Word**" and "**Jesus**"

The most important thing in marriage, as it is in all of life, is that we keep God's commandments! You did not meet your mate by chance. Your marriage is a part of Gods plan for your life! And God don't make mistakes! God has not changed His laws and principles to suit mankind! God laws remain true even today. And everything serves His plans, not ours! Praise God and Thank God for His mercy and for His love that is everlasting!

Keep Gods Commandment of marriage! Husbands keep your wives and wives keep your husbands. Stop letting Satan take your joy, destroying marriages, your lives and your families!

Audrey F. Evans-Ford

The Walk

One Sunday the Church sermon was about taking a walk. Taking time out for yourself and Jesus. Just get away from it all, the hustle and bustle of life. Take a walk and get in touch with the Divine Savior. You know in life when things get hectic we are often told to do things such as; "If the heat is to hot, then get out of the kitchen or take a walk a cool off!" This is good advice and in many cases has been proven to be right. True you cool off and even calm down. But you still are going back to the same situation with probably the same thinking. Well, I have some advice that I know bring you peace. Take a walk and talk with Jesus. Jesus will change everything, including your thinking.

I have a friend that I love so much. We use to get high together, smoking cocaine. It was on a Sunday morning, he had been out all night, elsewhere getting high. He came by early one Sunday morning all torn a part and hurting. He was hurting real bad, all he and I could do was hold each other and cry. He was tired. He was tired of the drugs and the life that he was living. He knew there had to be a better life for him, other than the one that he has been living. He told me that he was leaving. I mean leaving, leaving the State. He had to get away from this life of hell. Praise God! He did!

My friend did not own a car, bicycle or tricycle. But, this did not stop him from leaving. He borrowed a bicycle out of my garage. And peddled as far North as he could, until the bike got a flat tire. Then he began to walk, he walked for a long distance, eventually catching rides from one point to another. But, the biggest part of his journey was on foot. He walked. I spoke to a few of his family members about what had happened. I really was looking for some kind of compassion and love for him to be shown. It did not happen. They showed none, they laughed about it and made a joke about his source of travel. It was a joke to them.

Well, he did it. He made it to the next State by bicycling, hitchhiking and walking. During his travel, he became closer to Jesus and accepted Jesus as Lord over his life. He realized that Jesus is his savior. When my friend reached his destination, he was reconciled

Acknowledge, Beware and Recognize

with people that live according to Gods principles and laws. People that know, love, honor and respect God. My friend became closer to God and God came closer to him. It is written in

James 4:8-10, "Draw nigh to God, and he will draw nigh to you. Cleanse your hands, ye sinners; and purify your hearts, ye double minded. Be afflicted, and mourn, and weep; let your laughter be turned to mourning, and your joy to heaviness. Humble yourselves in the sight of the Lord, and he shall lift you up!"

My friend had been afflicted with drugs. His laughter turned into mourning and his joy had become a burden of heaviness. And these are the things that bought him to his knees and he humbled himself in the presence of God. And God kept his promise, God lift him up! God rescued him from his enemies and healed him of his drug affliction. My friend is now married with children! I know what you are thinking. You are thinking "What a Happy Ending!" Nope! Not quite yet.

Remember why I have written this book. I have written this book to help you hopefully to Acknowledge and recognize Satan 'works'. Sure God kept his promise to my friend as he does for all of us. But, there was still one problem. Satan does not give up! Satan don't care how close you get to God he is still going to attack you! Don't you know by now that Satan is determined to destroy Gods children and take away their blessings?

After my friend had accepted God in his life and was doing well. He came back to visit his family and I. When the visit was over and he was leaving, he and I were talking about Satan. My friend made a statement that really disturbed me. I immediately said to myself, "Oh no, he should not have said that!" A chill of fear ran through me for my friend! My friend said to me, "I am not worried about Satan, I am covered in the oil. When Satan try to grab me I will slip through his hands because I am covered in oil." Okay this part was all right with me, but he went farther than that, he said, "In fact, I challenge Satan to bother me!" Oh my God! What has my friend gone and done now? I knew what he did. He challenged an attack from Satan. And he got it!

I do not quite remember if it was a few weeks or a few months later. But, the attack was on. Satan attacked my friend. My friend having being reconciled with God fearing people meet and married a woman whose father is a Minister of the word. Now, even though my friend has accepted Jesus in his life, he had not quite shade off all of his old sinful nature. He was not honest about his past when he and his wife talked about it. He neglected to tell her about his past drug use. BAM! Satan got him! In fact Satan had a hold on him all along, Satan was just waiting for the right time to use his hold card. My friend challenged Satan and Satan attacked him, using his hold card, "The Deceit!"

My friend wife called worried about him and looking for him. She was so upset. Satan was working on her to! He was putting all kinds of thoughts in her head, especially the one of adultery. Every woman's worst nightmare! But, I convinced her, with the truth, no her husband was not with another woman. I know him just that well, he is not a womanizer, he is a faithful man and he does not, as some folk would say, "mess around!" I had an idea about what could have possibly happened and what he was probably doing. But I did not know it for a fact.

I still do not know it for a fact, but I think he backslide into the drug use for those few days, that he could not be found. The truth of his past drug use was revealed, because of this. His marriage was saved and healed. Because he came clean and told her the truth and as it is written in Psalm 91:9 my friend "hast made the LORD, which is his (our) refuge, even the most High, thy habitation; There shall no evil befall thee, nigh shall any plague come nigh thy dwelling. God loves, protects and saves his children! God has given his angels charge over us in our going and coming!

This story is to warn you not to "Don't Challenge Satan!" But, to acknowledge, recognize and beware of him! I am telling you again, "Do Not Challenge Satan!" Let God handle Satan, you can't! And don't even try to fool yourself that you can!

Let Go and Let God! Take "The Walk!" And praise God!

Acknowledge, Beware and Recognize

PSALM 124

If the Lord had not been on my side when people rose up against me,

They would have swallowed me alive because of their burning anger against me.

The waters would have engulfed me; a torrent would have overwhelmed me.

Yes, the raging waters of their fury would have overwhelmed my very life.

Blessed be the Lord, who did not let their teeth tear me apart!

I escaped like a bird from a hunter's trap.

The trap is broken, and I am free!

My help is from the Lord, who made the heavens and the earth!

Audrey F. Evans-Ford

The Comforter

One Sunday after Church I went to visit a neighbor. I had meet her once before and it had been awhile since I had seen her. I went to ask her where was a Church in the neighbor that I could go to for Bible study during the week. We begin talking about Jesus and the word and our love for Him. Then she asked me to come go to Church with her that evening. I told her maybe some other time, because I had just gotten home from Church. She gave to me the information that I wanted.

When she got home from Church that night, she called me on the phone and asked me if I could come over to her house the next day because God had something that He wanted to give me. I said sure.

So, the following day I went over to her house and she and I were talking, yes, about Jesus. Then she told me that a friend was coming over and did I mind having prayer service with them, I said okay, I would love too!

In the prayer service we begin praying giving thanks to God and praying for one another. Then we read through a pamphlet, "A Place Prepared for You." In this pamphlet was information about the Holy Spirit. Each of us took turns reading and discussing it. Afterwards we talked about the receiving of the Holy Spirit. Then we went into prayer again.

This time in praying, the ladies were telling me that the Holy Spirit was upon me. And to go ahead and speak in tongue, the Holy Spirit wanted me to pray in this new language that He had given to me. This baffled me. I just could not grasp what I should do. Well, they were praying and crying, and so was I, they were praying and crying and telling me to speak the Holy Ghost language, telling me "do it!" I was praying and crying because I was not receiving what they said I had received. So I begin to mimic them.

The following night I went to Bible study with them. Before Bible services begin people go into rooms to pray, these rooms are called prayer rooms. I went into one of the prayer rooms and I prayed and I cried and I Thanked God for loving me and showing me favor. People were praying, crying and speaking in tongue. Then again my prayer partners from the day before started telling me again to speak the language of the Holy Ghost! And as I begin to mimic them once more, the Spirit within me spoke and said no!

No, I had not been given the gift to speak in tongue and I am not to mimic the Holy Spirit. It is a sin to pretend or to mimic the Holy Spirit just to please someone! I had begin to get a headache, then I realized what was happening to me and as I realized what was happening the Spirit of God said to me, "Peace, be still." When my prayer partners started nudging me again to speak the language that had not been given to me I told them, "God said to me, "Peace and for me to be still" and I sat down in a chair and did just that.

I would like for you to think about this, "Have you ever prayed and received a headache?" I have never before in my life prayed and I have prayed for long periods of time, but I had never gotten a headache from praying! This night in the prayer room, being nudged to speak in tongue, about to attempt to mimic the Spirit, I immediately recognized the work of Satan. Satan is everywhere, even in prayer rooms and he tries to sliver his way into your prayers! He was in the prayer room telling me to mimic the Holy Spirit!

Jesus said in Matthew 12:31-32 "Every sort of sin and blasphemy will be forgiven men, but the blasphemy against the Spirit will not be forgiven. To fake, pretend or mimic the Holy Spirit is blasphemy and it is a sin." And Jesus said it, "You will not be forgiven!" Not ever! Satan tried to get me to commit the sin that he know that God will not forgive me for! Oh, but my God is an Awesome God, He knew what Satan was trying to do and He stopped it! Praise God! God said to me, "Peace, be still" I will never forget those words!

I know that God loves me and I know that His Spirit lives in me. I do not have to shout, jump up and down, scream and holler or mimic utterances of the Holy Spirit to prove anything to anyone. I have even been told to ask God for the gift to speak in tongue, because it gives power. Well, I almost fell for that too!

One morning when I woke up, I fell to my knees and begin to pray. I remembered listening to a ministry and being told to ask God for the gift to speak in tongue. As I was praying and asking God for the gift to speak in tongue, it hit me, like a ton of bricks, Audrey what are you doing? Do you know what a gift is? Yep! The serpent, Satan himself slivered his way in again. Oh, he is determined to cause me to stumble and fall, but Satan is a liar!

Sure, I know what a gift is. Example, my husband brought me a van. It was a gift. I did not ask him for it. There was no sign or anything indicating that he was buying it, and even lesser sign that he was getting it for me! When I realized what I was praying and asking of God, I stopped! I immediately asked God for His forgiveness. How dare I ask Him for such a gift! This is just my personal feeling, I would much rather received this awesome and powerful gift from God through His grace! Not my asking!

If or when I receive this wonderful gift that so many people speak of, I will receive it as I received the van from my husband. I will receive it unexpectedly and not asking for it! It is a "Gift!" To receive the Holy Spirit and the gift to speak in tongue is given to you freely from God. You do not have to ask for it. In John 14:15-17 Jesus tells us "If you love me, you will observe my commandments; and I will request the Father and He will give you another helper to be with you forever, the spirit of the truth, which the world cannot receive, because it neither beholds it nor knows it. You know it, because it remains with you and is in you. I shall not leave you bereaved."

God's Holy Spirit lives in us. We did not have to pray and ask God to fill us with His Spirit! It is by His grace the we have been filled with the Holy Spirit. And it is by the grace of God that we will receive the gift to speak the Holy Spirit Language. It is God's gift that He freely gives!

Again I am telling you to beware and recognize the works of Satan. Satan enters your prayers too! Satan hates our Comforter, the "Holy Spirit!"

Why Have Faith In God?

Oh yeah, Satan causes many of us to question God and to wonder why should we have faith in God. Especially after we have done wrong, knowing that we have sinned. Being children of God we believe and know that we are forgiven for our sins. But in fear of Gods judgment and feeling unworthy and undeserving of Gods mercy, we often lose faith in trusting God to forgive us and to answer our prayers. Let me tell you, don't ever lose faith in God, when you start thinking this way, it is an attack of Satan! Satan is attacking your mind, rubbing your sin in your face, reminding you of your sin and causing you to feel guilty and unworthy.

Listen Satan really is a "LIAR!" and there is no truth in him! In the Bible in John 8:44 we are told that, "Satan was a manslayer when he began and he did not stand fast in the truth, because the truth is not in him. When he speaks the lie, he speaks according to his own disposition, because he is a liar and the father of lies!" So what I am saying to you is, "Stop listening to Satan and stop letting him fill your mind with his lies!"

Jesus assures you (us) that if you (we) have faith and believe that whatever you (we) pray and ask for that you (we) will receive, then you (we) shall have it! This is written in Mark 11:22. It has been approximately three years since God has called me to write this book. But, I kept on being that bad, bad, bad little Audrey who did not want to grow up! I kept being disobedient to God and would not answer His call. Guess what? God did not forsaken me, He did for me what my natural Mom did for me. God gave me enough rope to hang myself! And yep! I hung myself, big time! Ignoring God bought me to my knees and had me calling Him!

My almighty Father God did not have to take me across His knee to discipline me. He just looked at me and watched me act like a fool, living in sin! God knew that I would fall. He was right there just waiting and when I fell He picked me up, wiped the scares clean and nursed me until I was healed. He forgave me for being disobedient. He forgave me for not living according to His laws and principles. He had mercy on me and gave me His grace! Let me tell you after that last fall of mine, loosing everything and everyone in my life. I hurried up and repented. I humbled myself under the Almighty Hands of My Father God and I accept Jesus Christ as my Savior.

Why should you have faith in God? "Why should'nt you?" Ask yourself, "What has Satan done for you lately?" What has Satan ever done for you other than lie to you, deceive you, causing you pain and suffering, destroying your life? Why not have faith in God! Jesus says in John 8:46, "That He speaks the truth and whoever does not believe Him is convicting Him of sin!" Are you calling the Son of God a sinner and a liar?

You need to know that the reason you should have faith in God is because it is written in John 1:1 that, "In the beginning was the Word, and the Word was with God, and the Word was God!" It is Gods word that gave to you life. It is also written in Isaiah 55:11 that Jesus says that His word that goes forth from His mouth, will prove to be. It will not return to Him void, but that it will certainly do that in which He have delighted and it will have certain success in that for which He have sent it!

Jesus said to, "To keep asking, and it will be given you; keep on seeking, and you will find; keep on knocking and it will be opened to you. For everyone asking receives and everyone seeking finds, and to everyone knocking it will be opened." And this is written in Matthew 7:7-8. Oh and you better believe it, God watches over His word to perform it! God wants you to ask anything that you will of Him so the His word will prove to be! You doubt Him? You don't have faith! Then ask Him! He wants you to and I dare you to!

I did not deliberately test Gods word because I do fear Him. But, I can say even though not deliberate, I tested God and His word, and it has proven to be, with success! I asked God for His forgiveness and I received it! I asked God to heal me and I am healed. I asked God to give me back my life with Jesus, and He did! Thank You Father! I repented and humbled myself under Our Almighty Father Gods' hand! I am being obedient to His laws and live according to His principles. And I am also being abundantly blessed!

Have "Faith" in God, because God word is alive! God word is truth! God word will never return to Him void! It is Gods word that we even "Exist!" It is written in Exodus 9:16 that God says, "**He has kept us in existence, for the sake of showing us His power and in order to have His name declared in all the earth!**"

Isn't this a good enough reason to "**Have Faith In God?**"
He that is from God listens to the sayings of God!
John 8:47

Audrey F. Evans-Ford

D *evil attacking*
O *ur minds causing*
U *s not to*
B *elieve and*
T *rust in God!*

When Am "I" Important?

Never! Never am I important! You see, when we start to feel or even think that we are important, we begin to feel as though we are as important or as great as God!

I was not created to be important, I was created in Gods image to love Him, to serve Him and to be "**Humble**," not important. It is important for me to know I am Gods Child.

The only important person I know is the Great I Am, Our Father God Himself! "And God said to Moses, "I AM THAT I AM" Who is important? Not, I, but the great "I AM" my creator, Our Father!

Whenever man starts to feel important, he needs to know that he is being used as Satan's weapon against God! Satan knows that when man begins to feel important, he wants to be praised and honored like God! Don't Do It! You see what happened to Satan!

Satan wants you to become vain and do what he did, dishonor God! Satan is trying to make you feel important so that you will feel just as powerful, great and as important as God! Don't Do It!

Yes, we are important, we are important to God! We are His children, His heirs and His image! In the book of Genesis it is written "And **God** proceeded to "**create**" the **man in His image!**" Not be Him! Nor take His place!

Audrey F. Evans-Ford

The Pop Quiz

How many of you can remember back in your school days, going to class and have gotten comfortable in your seat, then your teacher tells you to put everything in your desk, "We are having a "Pop Quiz" today!"

Quite a few of us became unraveled and panicked. We were nervous and some of us became frightened. I know because I was one of them that panicked many times. I would become frightened especially when I knew that I had been fooling around in class and had not been paying attention.

Believe it or not, Life is based on this very same principle as the "Pop Quiz." Yes, we are tested everyday of lives. There are many of us who do not see it this way. But, it is true. As Christians, we are in class all of the time. We are living on campus, in the word and we are in Jesus classroom day and night! Are we paying attention and learning? Are we ready for a 'Pop Quiz"?

Our four majors in the "Word College of Jesus" are: Awareness, Faith, Strength and Courage. And a "Pop Quiz" is always given in theses subjects. So, just a small piece of advice, from someone who knows, "Don't fool around in Jesus class!" you do not want to fail!

I have failed the pop quiz many, many times. Thank God, Jesus did not kick me out of school! Praise the Lord! Let me tell you about one pop quiz that I did fail. One day my cousin and I, along with a friend of his, had to take my sister to the airport in North Carolina. The trip itself was fairly comfortable and a little enjoyable. It would have been a lot more enjoyable if it had not been for Satan deciding to take the trip with us to. I realized that Satan had taken the trip with us when my cousin asked me, "So, what are you now?" He was referring to me trying to live my life right in Christ. My reply to him was "I am a sinner." He responded by saying, "Oh, okay, I just wanted to know." We finally made to the airport, guess what? My sister missed her flight. Yeah, Satan had targeted us this day, especially me!

My pop quiz was on "Awareness." Did I pass it? Sure I did, I was aware of Satan attacking me. Satan was working me over this day. You see, I had just recently made up my mind and I was and I still am today, determine to live my life according to the laws and principles of God! Anyway, knowing this, Satan was having a field day with me. I was constantly being caught off guard with God. I had begun using profanity and I mean a lot of it! I would catch myself every time and ask for forgiveness immediately. This brought shame to me, to be caught off guard with God and have no control of my tongue!

Whew! What a day. Satan did not stop there. When I returned home that night, Satan worked on me again. At this time my husband and I were separated, the work of Satan again. I tried to get in touch with my husband to let him know that I was back home. The truth is I wanted to see him. He was nowhere to be found. And of course, this upset me greatly. I could not sleep a wink. I went to the chapel and prayed. I went back home and prayed. I watched the spiritual television all night. And still, I found no peace. I was wondering not some much where he was, but who was he with. Was he with another woman? Sure he was. Satan had roll call and I was on his list.

The following morning I was just through, I had become weak battling with Satan all night. I went to my friend and I told her what had happened. And I cried until I became sick. She talked to me. Then we went to the chapel together. When we returned to her place, we talked again. Oh, she and I talked all day long. She talked to me until I felt better!

Shirley knew that I had made up my mind to live my life in the word. And she knew without a doubt that it was Satan attacking me. Then it hit me like a ton of bricks. Oh, Thank God! I had been given a "Pop Quiz"! This was a test of my sincerity! Satan was pushing all my buttons to see if I would give up and change my mind about living my life in and for Jesus! Hate it for you, Satan. I love my Lord and Savior Jesus Christ and I am determined to live my life according to His word and His principles. And I will!

Thank God, I passed the "Pop Quiz" that Satan gave to me on my "Sincerity" to God! Yes, I am determined to live according to the word of my God! However, I did fail my test on "Strength." I had let Satan beat me down. But, God picked me right back up!

I say all of this to you hoping that you pass your "Pop Quiz" in "Awareness." Whenever you are having a "not so good day" remember to be aware, it is only Satan at work. You must be aware of Satan at all times. Satan does not take a break. Satan is waiting for you to take a break! Stay on "Guard with God!"

Be a straight "A" student (servant) for God!

Audrey F. Evans-Ford

"Love Thy Enemy!"

I know that you have probably heard this all of your life, "Love thy enemy." I know that at times this has probably been very hard for many of us to do. And in many cases we did buried the hatched and forgave one another and moved on. This is all good! Now here is something for you to think about! How are you supposed to feel about your enemy, our greatest adversary, the Devil! Are we supposed to love him too?

It is written in Romans 13:10 that love does not work evil, love is the law of God fulfilled. Therefore, we are told in Colossians 3:14 to cloth ourselves with love for it is a perfect bond and union with God. And it is written in 1 Corinthians 15:25 that our Father God subject all things, (including) all our enemies (as well as the Devil!) under his feet.

Well how about the Devil? Are we supposed to love Him? Yes! Why? The Devil is our greatest enemy. He is the one that is seeking to destroy and kill us! Why should we love him? Why?

Because, the Devil does not want us to! He wants us to hate him! He wants us to break Gods commandment of love. It is written in Matthew 22:44 that Gods' greatest law is the law of love! Be aware of the Devils' lies, he has been around for a very, very long time. Remember he started his mess in heaven and got kicked out! Sure, God became angry with Lucifer, but not once have you ever read or have been told that God hated Lucifer, even after he had become evil.

It is very important that you do not have any hate in your heart towards anything and anyone. I do not care what the Devil does to you, do not hate him, it is a trick to steal your soul. This is why I have told you in this book about some of Satan's weapons. Satan use his weapons of anger, bitterness, envy, hostility and jealousy to hopefully cause you to hate. Don't do it!

Satan wants you to get angry. He knows that once you build up enough anger that you will eventually began to hate. Again I am telling you don't do it! It is a trick to get you to break Gods commandment and fall back into sin. So watch out! Yes, you will become frustrated, irritated and tired of Satan attacks on your life. Don't worry God is watching over you and protecting you.

Acknowledge, Beware and Recognize

Let me tell you what I have learned since I have surrendered my life to Christ. I realize that Satan is very angry with me for leaving his world and surrendering my life to Jesus. Now he is attacking me constantly. For example, Satan is using my husband David against me. David has done and said many cruel and nasty things to me. But, it is okay. I know that it is the work of Satan. Satan wants me to hate David. But, guess? I love David even more, because I realize what is happening to him. Instead of being angry with David I continue to love him and I pray for him. I Bless David, I do not curse him. David is not the only one that Satan uses against me. He uses other members of my family too! And guess what? I love them even more than before and I pray for them and I Bless them too! I realize that Satan refuses to let go without a fight and he is determined to make me fall or at least stumble.

Let me tell something I do not care what Satan does or who he uses to attack and hurt me, 'I WILL NOT HATE THEM!' I will not curse them! I will love them, pray for them and I will continue to Bless them. You see, I understand what Jesus meant before He died on the cross and asked our Father to "forgive them, they know not what they do!" I myself have hurt and wronged many people and I am truly sorry for what I have done. I realize that I did not know what I was doing. If I had known Jesus then like I know Him now, I would not have done those things. I asked God to please help all those whom I have ever hurt, wrong, done an evil to and caused to suffer, those whom I have persecuted and had a cruel attitude towards to please release and forgive me! Yes, I am sorry for any wrong that I have done to anyone. And I also ask God to release and forgive all those who have wronged and hurt me. I forgive and release them because I understand that it is the work of Satan!

Look, it is very important that you and I have no bitterness, envy, strife, or any unkindness in us in any form. It is not of God. It is the work of Satan. It is important for me to stress to you that Satan is not going to let up. He is going to continue to attack you. It is his job to cause you to be bitter, jealous, angry, hostile, whatever it takes to make you hate!

I know that Satan is very angry with me for surrendering my life to Christ and living according to Gods' laws and principles and he is trying to cause me to stumble and fall. Satan is doing everything and whatever he can to cause me to stumble and fall! But, I am determined not too fall! I have been there and done that and I am determined not to go there again.

I came up with a way for me to deal with Satan attacks. Maybe this way will help you too! I had to get a new attitude! I thought about it one day, I was truly getting aggravated and frustrated with the Devil messing with me. I said to myself this is enough, Satan I am sick of you. I was not angry, I was just sick of him. He was beating me down and wearing me down, just making me tired and weak, taking my energy! I mean his attacks were interfering with my praying, my emotions and my writing. Oh no, this fool has got to go! Then it hit me! This fool just won't quit.

Then, I remembered reading in the Holy Bible how Jesus handled the Devil. Jesus did not get angry at the Devil. He calmly rebuked the Devil. Jesus simply told the Devil what to do and the Devil obeyed. Jesus did not get angry at demons, he simply told them what to do, and they obeyed. Everything that I had read in the scriptures started coming to mind. The Holy Spirit was talking to me, telling me how to handle the Devil! Thank You Lord Jesus!

I was reminded that it is He (The Holy Spirit of God) that is within me that is greater than he (The Devil) that is in the world. Being made the righteous of Our Father through Jesus shed blood upon the cross means that I am heir to all that belongs Our Father God. I have also been given Authority over all the power of the enemy. Jesus says in Matthew 18:18 that "Whatever things you (I) may bind on earth in His name will be bound in heaven and whatever things that you (I) lose on earth in His name is loosed in heaven!" this means that we (I) have the victory over Satan. I have the authority, power and strength to bind, rebuke and resist the Devil!

I remembered every promise that Jesus made and His promise is fixed in my heart and in my mind. I remembered that it is written in Isaiah 55:11 that Jesus said that His word goes forth from His mouth will prove to be. He said that His word will not return to Him without results with a certain success! And yes, I believe Jesus! Jesus was attentive to my prayers as a sinner and answered me, so I know that He surely will answer my prayer as His righteousness one. I have right standing with Our Father. His Holy Spirit lives in me. I am assured and confident that I have authority over all the power of the enemy, the Devil!

Acknowledge, Beware and Recognize

I acknowledge the fact that Satan does not sleep and he does not get tired and neither does Jesus! Jesus knows that at times the Devil beats on us to the point where we get tired and feel like giving up. This is why Jesus has given to us dynamic energy. Jesus wants us to be fully abound in power (against Satan) and this is written in the book of Isaiah 40:29.

You do not have to get angry with Satan nor hate him when he is attacking you, tormenting you. Think about this, how does the Devil attack you? He attacks your mind and sometimes your body. But he mostly attacks your mind. The Devil tricks are not new. They are the same old ones that he always uses. Check this out! Satan can do only the things that you and God allow him to do. Satan did not give you life and he sure cannot take it! Ask God!

You need to know that Satan plans to have field day, everyday with your mind and with your heart. Causing you to hate one another and even question God! Now take a little time and think about this. Why do we let Satan torment us causing our hearts to be troubled and sometimes filled with hate knowing that he is trying to destroy us?

We must be aware of Satan lies, deceit and tricks. We must prepare ourselves for Satan attacks like we prepare ourselves for a "fire drill." (After all, Hell is a Lake of Fire!) Remember how schools and businesses have fire drills to prepare us for a fire. They show us ways to escape the fire. Well this is the same principle that I am talking about when it comes to Satan. We have to prepare to escape Hells fire! Reading this book is one way, reading the Holy Bible is another way, but becoming intimate with God is the best way! We must be prepared for Satan's attacks. We do this with the word of God and the Authority that we have been given over the power of the enemy. It is written in the book of Acts 1:8 that this 'POWER' that we have in us is **beyond what is normal to man** because **it is neither of you nor man, it is of God!**

Do not ever "Hate!" I have not read nor have I ever heard that God hated anything or anyone. God loves all of His creations, yes including Satan. Sure God cast Lucifer down from heaven, but not once has it ever been said that God hated him. Remember Satan was not always the Devil; he was once God favorite angel, Lucifer. Lucifer waged war in heaven because he wanted his own kingdom. This world that we live in is (Satan's) his kingdom and God allows him to rule it. Does this sound like God hate Lucifer even though he turned against Him?

Don't hate Satan. Just bind, rebuke and resist him. And "Put on the complete suit of armor of God that you maybe able to stand firm against the machinations (Lies and deceptions) of the Devil. The Bible tells us in Ephesians 6:11 that "God does not want us to have "hate" any place in us! God does not want us to hate anyone, not even Satan!

The law of **LOVE** is the fulfillment of life in Jesus Christ! And we are to continually subject ourselves to God and oppose the Devil. We are not to allow any place in us for the Devil to dwell. And we are told in James 4:7 to "Keep Our Senses and Be Watchful." Yes, keep our senses because Satan loves to attack our mind.

When Satan attacks your mind with impure, evil, sinful or negative thoughts, "Stop" him! Focus on God! It is written in Colossians 3:2 for us to "KEEP YOUR MIND FIXED ON THE THINGS ABOVE! and not on the things upon this earth." Remember we must not "**Hate!**"

"Communicate with God, and Love thy enemy, even Satan!

"GOD NEVER LEFT AND GOD NEVER LEAVES!"

I Said I Can't!

How many times have I said, "God I can't do it!" I said God, I am not strong enough, I am too weak. And God just look down upon me and smiled. He put His loving arms around me and said to me, "No my child you can't, but you will because I will strengthen you and help you!"

I kept telling God, "God I am not like Job." If I were to lose all of what little that I have, my husband, my children and my family I would go crazy and probably die! God said to me, "no you won't, you are as strong as Job." God let me know that even though I was not righteous like Job, I am still His child and that He loves me just as much as He loves Job. God said that He would not and will not let the Devil take my soul! I lost all that I had, my husband, a place to live, my children and my family! Thank God, I still have my soul!

Then I said to God one day, "God, you showed King David so much love and mercy, forgiving him for his sins and blessing him, don't you love me as much as you love King David?" I said, "God, King David even had his mistress husband killed and you forgave him. I never killed anyone or had anyone killed. Don't you love me as you loved King David?"

God once again put his arms around me showing me that He does love me and He said to me, "Audrey, I love you too, I love you just as I love all my children, and yes, I love you just as much as I love King David! I have shown you favor and I will continue to show you favor, I know your heart and I know your love for me!" God opened my eyes and my heart to see that He does love me. He showed me that He loves all of His children equally, but yet, differently. Our Father God is righteous and judges us accordingly. His judgment is always fair! And so is His discipline!

It is written in Psalm 91:14-16 God says, "He will rescue those who love Him. He will protect those who trust in His name. When they (we) call on Him, He will answer. He will be with those in trouble. God will rescue us. He will satisfy us with a long life and give to us His salvation!" He will do it!

I called God. God heard me, and He answered me. God lifted me from the pit of darkness. He renewed my mind and created a clean heart within me. I love Him and I trust Him. Sure, I was allowed to suffer for a while. I needed to be disciplined. But, through it all Jesus rearranged my life and made me a better person!

God kept His promises to me. He said call Him and I did. Thank You Father God, I said, "I can't!" and you said to me; "You can and you will!" Yes, "I CAN and I WILL!" I did not die! I have been given a new life! Thank you Jesus! Thank you Father God!

Don't! Give up

I really do not consider myself to be an authority much. However, I am a living witness to the wonderful works of our Father God! And I know first hand that His word will always prove to be! I have suffered much and there may come a time that I may suffer again. Thank God for His love and His word. When I had lost all hope and was about to give up, it was Gods' word that kept me from giving up! It is the word of God that has given me life and strength!

One morning while I was watching several Television ministries, I realized that most of our problems are people related. It is our relationships with others that have a lot to do with the way we live and how we live our lives. Rather it be Mom, Dad, sister, brother, spouse, children, co-workers, etc... unfortunately many of our lives seem to be destined by the lives of others in our life. I know, it happened to me for forty-nine years!

I wanted to give up on life for two reasons, one of the reasons is that I loved the people in my life so much, that I wanted to please them but I never could. The other reason that I wanted to give up on life is because I was a shame. I had put everyone first in my life, instead of God. I had broken the number one golden rule: "You must love God with all your heart, your soul and your mind!" And this is written in the book of Matthew 22:37. Yes, we must love God our Father with our entire being! And I did'nt! My love for the people in my life was greater than my love for God. Especially for my husband!

I spent my life giving love and looking for love never finding it. And because I could not find it I was living a reckless and sinful life! No one really accepted me. They put up with me when it was beneficial to them, other than that no one really wanted to be bothered with me! Let me put it this way, the ones that I wanted to be bother with, did not want to be bother with me. I was always doing something wrong, talked about and judged by them. They would wait and watch to see what I would do wrong next. It was the rejection of those I dearly love, that pushed me to my Father God. And I am so glad that they rejected me. Rejecting me was the best things that they could have ever done for me! I did not know that I was doing anything wrong loving those people in my life the way that I did. I always knew that the greatest gift that God had given to me was love. But, I guess I did not fully understand this thing about love.

I knew and have always known that love is the greatest Gift that God gave man. This is why I have always loved my children, my family members and my husband with my whole heart. It is written in 1 Peter 4:8 that we are to, "Above all things **have intense love for one another**, because love covers a multitude of sins." This is true! Well my love for my husband and my family was very intense! My knowledge about love was limited and slack because I was living in sin. Satan blocked me from obtaining the true knowledge of how to love and where to place my love! Love has to be placed in its proper place. Putting God First! Then Husband, children, etc…

I did not know that I was sinning against God. I thought I was doing exactly what God had wanted me to do. I was not breaking Gods commandments about having any other gods before Him. I made no graven image of Him. I have not and will not bow down nor serve any other gods. I don't even believe in any other gods. Well all that was and is good, but the knowledge of loving God my Father with my entire being, had been blocked and kept me from knowing how important it is that I love my Father God with my entire being. Satan did not want me to know that! Well now I know it, Hallelujah! Hallelujah! Thank you Jesus! Now I know!

If the problem in your life is because of someone that you love, then ask yourself, "Do I love this person more than I love God? If your answer is yes, then you know the solution to your problem. "GOD!" I made the honest mistake of loving my husband more than I loved God and myself. There were always problems and now we are not together. Satan knew what he was doing. Satan knows that anyone and anything that you love more than God, you will lose! I thank God for His awesome and unfailing love and for forgiving me for my ignorance!

God has spoken into my life and said for me not to give up on my marriage, but to commit it into His mighty hands. He will fix it!

Listen, you do not have to give up your dreams nor your desires! The only thing that you ever need to give up is sin! And begin by loving Our Father God with your entire being! Just love Him!

Let me tell you something else. It does not matter what your problem is, no matter how bad the situation or circumstances may 'appear' to be, put God first in your life and **Love God with your entire being!** Watch our Father God perform miracles in your life. Watch God make what you think is impossible, possible! Trust God and God alone, never man!

Whatever or whoever your problem is, "**Don't Give Up**" just simply "**Let Go And Let God!**"

Audrey F. Evans-Ford

Words of Encouragement from Psalm 37

Trust in the Lord and do good. Commit everything you do to Him. Trust Him and He will help you.

Day by day the Lord takes care of His children. They will survive through hard times. Though they stumble, they will not fall, for the Lord holds them by the hand. The Lords children have never been forsaken.

So, don't worry about the wicked. Don't envy those who do wrong. Stop your anger! Turn from your rage! It only leads to harm.

Turn from evil and do good. For in a little while the wicked will disappear. You will look for them they will be gone. Like springtime flowers, they soon wither and are gone. The Lord will not let the wicked succeed.

Don't be impatient for the Lord to act! Just travel steadily along His path. Live according to Gods principles and obey His laws. He will honor you, giving to you whatever your heart desires.

The Lord loves justice and He will never abandon you! He will keep you safe!

You will see the wicked "DESTROYED!"

Praying

All praise to God our Father and Christ Jesus! I have just gotten off the telephone talking to my baby brother Kyle. I was telling him that the Holy Spirit had given me a story to write. I was telling him about how I have heard people say ask others to pray for you. Then I begin to tell him that I had reservations about asking others to pray for me, because I have also heard people say, do not ask other to pray for you because you do not know what they are praying for you. They might be praying against you! My brother surprised me. He said that if they are praying to God against me, don't worry about it! God does not accept or acknowledge prayers that are to hurt or harm anyone!

Praise God, my baby brother was used in my life to confirm what the Holy Spirit had already told me to write. God used my baby brother to confirm His instructions and reassured me that this is what He wanted me to write.

Moving on with what God has called me to write. Praying. There are so many people that feel like they do not know how to pray. Well listen to this, we all know how to ask for things when we want them or feel like we need them, don't we? Okay here is some very good news for you. We all know how to pray! We all do not pray in the same way. But, why would we, we are all different! We all have different needs and desires and we all have different relationships with God! Therefore, our prayers and the way we pray are different too!

First of all we must know what praying is! Do you know what praying is? Let me simplify what praying is for you. Praying is simply talking to God like you would talk to your best friend. Believe it or not, God is your best friend! Think about it, when you ask a friend for something, you just ask them for what you want. For example, I have heard men say to their fellow man, "man let me borrow a dollar!" that is asking a friend. The difference in asking God for what you want or need is that, you are asking our Father God who is Holy and the creator. Therefore your conversation with Him is called prayer.

There are many people that say that they do not know how to pray to God, if you are one of these people. I am here to tell you, yes you do. You know how to pray to God. If you can talk to a friend, a strange, a family member or a doctor about your problems and your desires, then you can talk (pray) to God! God already knows your heart and He knows your desires, your wants and your needs. God knows everything there is to know about you. He is just waiting to hear it from your mouth!

God wants you to be intimate with Him. He wants you to trust in Him. God is not just your Heavenly Father and creator, but your best friend as well. God wants you to talk to Him about your life, your problems and your desires. Let me tell you, putting your trust in man and not in God will surely bring many disappointing and painful situations into your life. Man cannot do for you what God can. Man will let you down and will not always be around!

I repeat Praying is simply talking to God. Talking to God is called praying because praying is prayer. Prayer is acknowledging God! Prayer is telling God that you know that He is our Father and our Creator. Prayer is giving God honor, glory and praise as we speak to Him!

God is Our Father, Our Creator and Our Best Friend. Whatever you say to Him will not be repeated. What goes on between you and God stays with you and God. He won't discuss what goes on between you and Him with no one. Whatever you asked God for He will give it to you. God will never let you down and He will always be around. Jesus Christ our Savior encourages us to pray to our Father. It is written in the book of Matthew 6:6 that we are to go into a private room or any place that is private and pray (talk) to Him in secret. He is there with you in secret and He will reward you and answer your prayers. God is waiting for you to talk to Him!

Oh and there is nothing wrong with asking other to pray for you. But, I strongly suggest that you establish a personal and intimate relationship with God yourself and this is done through prayer. Remember, praying is simply just talking to God. And believe this, no one can talk to God about your problems, your wants, your needs nor your desires better than you!

Check this out, the best thing about God being your best friend, is that He loves you unconditionally and He is always faithful and give to you whatever you ask of Him, and He gives it to you freely!

**********Talk To God!**********

Acknowledge, Beware and Recognize

S *atan's*
H *ostile*
A *ttempt to prevent*
M *any of us from praying and having*
E *verlasting life!*

Audrey F. Evans-Ford

"Soul" What is it?

December 1, 2001 is a day that I will never, ever forget. It took me forty-nine years to find out what the "Soul" is! I am serious! I had never really thought about my soul, nor the soul of man at all. Whenever I heard the "word" soul used, I basically just thought about it as a way of expressing or describing Black heritage. It was just a black thing to me. To me, 'Soul' was also a word used to reflect the Black Race, as a spiritual race of people that were meek and closer to God.

When I was coming up in the fifties, the sixties and the seventies, soul was used very often to describe Black peoples way of doing things. They danced with soul, meaning they danced with rhythm. They cooked soul food, black-eye peas, collard greens, cornbread and chitterlings. Their love and joy in cooking was from the soul, because of the deep love in their hearts for cooking. Their songs were soulful songs, songs sung deep down from within their hearts. They sung songs of faith and hope. They sung the blues, love songs, sad songs and yes, happy songs too!

Afros, Black Power and Black Panthers, Peace marches, etc… reflected "soul" people. The terminology 'Soul' was used to describe black people. Blacks were referred to as 'Soul People' because they praised, worshipped and trusted God no matter what, with all their heart and "Souls." Black People were Spiritually Strong!

I have been taught about Jesus all of my life. I remember being taught about His birth, His life, His suffering, His death and His resurrection. I do not remember being taught anything about our soul or about a soul at all. So I never thought about my soul or Jesus soul. I was seeking information in the Bible in reference to one of my other stories and I came across this information about the soul. In Matthew 20:28 it is written that when Jesus was talking to His disciples about ministering the word. Jesus said that He did not come into the world to be ministered to, but to minister and that He also came to give His "SOUL" as ransom in exchange for ours! Chills are running through me right now as I write this. In fact, I cried when I first read it. I know

now that I have a soul. I know that the blood that runs through my flesh and my veins is the 'Soul' of my body as well as my life!

It never crossed my mind that when Jesus died on the cross for me that He was giving up His soul. I just thought that He gave up life, itself, you know, His body died. I never connected the two, His soul and His body. At the last supper when Jesus broke the bread, He said, "This is my Body, which is given for you." I never gave any thought to His death other than His body being crucified, being put to death. I never thought about His "soul" or a soul at all. I had to get a better understanding of this. So, I read the Bible until I found the answer. Now, I am hoping that in some way that you will be enlightened also!

It is so awesome, it is not the life in our body that gets us into heaven or keeps us out, it is our "souls". You see, our bodies can be killed, but not our souls! In Matthew 10:28 Jesus tells us not to become fearful of those who kill the body but cannot kill the soul; but for us to fear him that can destroy both the soul and the body. And we know that that one is the Devil! Yap! Satan himself!

It is written in Genesis 1:20-21 that in the beginning when God created life, He created the waters and with His word He spoke unto the waters and told the waters to swarm forth living souls. God also spoke to the heavens bringing forth living souls. Every living creature is a living soul. And it is written in Genesis 2:7 that God proceeded to form the man out of dust from the ground and to blow into his nostrils the breath of life and the man came to be a living soul! Is'nt it wonderful how we have come to have a soul!

For those of you who do not have knowledge about the soul, I offer and share with you the knowledge that I have obtained. Are you ready for this?

"Our soul is the blood of our flesh." And think about it, our blood runs through every part of our flesh. There is no part of the flesh or the body that is untouched by blood. It is written in Leviticus 17:14 that, "**The soul** of every sort **of flesh is its blood**." Now that I understand what the soul is, I realize exactly what Jesus has done for me! He gave His soul for mine! At the Last Supper Jesus gave to His disciples a cup of wine and said to them "Drink this is my Blood, for the new covenant, which I shed for you and for many for the forgiveness of sin." The wine represents His blood, and His blood represents His soul! Jesus gave His 'Soul' for us!

It is by the word of God, that all living creatures have souls. It is the blood of all sort of flesh that is the soul of the temple (body) in which it flows. The soul of man is connected with the spirit of God. Just as blood flows through every part of the flesh and the body, so does the spirit of God. The spirit and the soul are one!

We are created in the image of God and it is by His word and spirit that we live! When God blew breath into man, He also blew into man His spirit! When God sent His Son into the world, He sent Him down by the power of His spirit! Jesus is the Son and Spirit of God! We are Gods creation, made in His image and we are His heirs and are partakers of His Spirit!

God our Father said in Ezekiel 18:4 that "All souls belongs to Him. Just as the soul of His Son Jesus Christ belongs to Him. God also knows all about the Devil and how the Devil seeks to destroy and kill His children. He knows that the Devil wants to steal our souls!

And it is for this reason that God sent His Son Jesus Christ into the world. To save our souls!

Jesus came to minister and to teach us the laws and principles of God. Jesus lived, suffered, was crucified, died, and rose again after death to fulfill the will of our Father God! Jesus hoped that we would come to our senses and take heed to His word and His death on the cross! Jesus told us in John 14:6 that He is the way and the truth and the life. No one comes to the Father except through Him.

Did you know that you have a soul? Have you acknowledged it yet? Have you become intimate with God? Do you want too? Do you want to save your soul?

Then you need to know that it is written in Acts 3:23 that, "Any soul that does not listen to the word of God will be completely destroyed from among God children!" and "What benefit will it be to you if you gain the whole world and forfeit your soul? Think about it.

To save your "SOUL" you must be obedient to the word of God. Obey His laws and live according to His principles. Stand firm and be strong. It is written in Deuteronomy 6:5 that "You must love God with all your hearts and with all your **soul**! Thank Jesus for ransoming His soul in exchange for yours!

"YOUR SOUL, WHERE WILL IT GO?"

Acknowledge, Beware and Recognize

Before I Exist No More

Oh, Jesus my Lord, my God I ask of thee please help me to be what you want me to be, before I exist no more.

Strengthen me and give to me the courage, the wisdom and the knowledge to do thy will.

Lord you have reminded me that my time here is brief. You have reminded me that my life is no longer than the width of my hand and that my days are numbered.

Lord Jesus yes, I confess that I have sinned against you and I am truly sorry and I humbly repent!

Lord Jesus, help me to abandon my sinful and shameful ways. Have mercy upon me and forgive me for my sins, before I exist no more.

Help me to serve you and live according to your laws and principles, doing only the things Lord that you would have me to do!

Spare me Lord Jesus and restore my life, let me smile again. I know that my life is no more than a breath to you!

Come quickly Lord Jesus, my life is fleeing! Come quick Lord, answer my prayers before I exist no more!

You Lord Jesus and you alone are my salvation!

AFFORD

Audrey F. Evans-Ford

Be Determined!

I have dedicated this book especially to drug users and abusers. The reason I have done this is because, I was a user and abuser of drugs. This book is also dedicated to every one who loves God and believes in Him, but yet has given up hope! You are reading this book because it is proof that God loves all of His children no matter what they have done! There is no sin that He will not forgive and no sickness He will not cure!

We are all Gods children and we are all heirs to all that belongs to Him. It does not matter what sin you have committed, knowingly or unknowingly. Jesus will forgive you. Remember that we are simply His sheep that went astray, that's all! Jesus knows what we are up against in this life. He knows our greatest adversary, the Devil. And even though we are all sinners, we all are His children. And it is written in the book of John 10:16 that Jesus says that He must bring us back. Jesus says that we will listen to His voice and we will become one flock, with one shepherd!

Sure, many of us have gone astray. It is okay. Jesus loves us and understands. He will forgive us and still bless us. But, yes, there is a but! The but is this, we must resist the Devil and turn our lives around by loving and accepting Him in our lives, doing the things that we know that He would have us to do. Doing the things that are righteous and the will of Our Father God! In other words be obedient to the laws of God and live according to His principles!

Those of us that are suffering because of drugs, sicknesses, lack of money, broken marriages, children rebelling, etc… I assure you that this is the work of Satan. The Devil is determined to steal, kill and destroy us. But we are blessed, because we belong to God our Father, who is the creator and He has His very own plan for us, this is why He sent His only begotten Son, Jesus into this world.

It is also written in the book of John 10:10 that the thief does not come unless it is to steal, kill and destroy. It is also written in the book of John that Jesus said that He had come that we might have life and might have it in abundance. Jesus is our shepherd; and He surrendered His soul on our behalf. Jesus said that His sheep listen to His voice and He knows them and they follow Him. Jesus gives to us everlasting life and by no means will we be destroyed and that there is nothing and no one that will snatch us out of His hand! You see, our Father God has given Jesus authority over all things.

Now knowing this, we need to be determined at some point and hopefully it is now, to be like Jesus and become His followers! Look, the Devil is determined to destroy us at whatever cost! He does not care what he has to do or what it will take to do it. You want to know why? Because his wages for sin has already been paid! He will spend eternity in hell and there is no way out for him! Satan has nothing to lose, absolutely nothing at all, but you do.

Thank God for our wonderful Savior Jesus Christ. We have a way out. Jesus paid the price for our sins, with His precious blood. Jesus willingly surrendered His life to death so that we might have everlasting life. But, the Devil has blind so many of us and deafened our ears to hear. Guess what? Jesus is not asking you or I to surrender our lives over to death. He has already done that for us. All Jesus is asking is that we commit our ways unto our Father and be obedient to His laws and live according to His principles.

But, like I just said, so many of us have become blind and deafened by the Devil. And there are many of us who do not want to listen to the word of God, because we do not want to give up the things of the world. We don't want promises. We live for today and the things that we can see, feel, touch and taste now! And Satan knows this!

And yes, Satan is determined to keep our ears deaf to the voice of God. But guess what? Jesus said that His sheep will listen to His voice. Meaning that if you belong to Jesus, no matter what the Devil does, you will hear Him! You can be right in the midst of sin and sinning and if Jesus decides to speak to you during that time, you will hear Him! I personally know this, been there and heard His voice! Let me tell you something, the Devil is powerless over God and He truly is powerless over you too! Check this out, even Satan himself has to listen to Jesus and obey!

The thing is this, we have to become as determined as the Devil! Yes, I said it **"BE AS DETERMINED AS THE DEVIL."** We must be as determined as the Devil and save our souls! He is determined to take them! Are you determined to keep your soul? I know that I am! I am for this reason only, happy to say that I have something in common with the Devil. Yes, determination! I am as determined to keep my soul as he is to take it! I love Jesus and I am determined to live according to God's principles and obey His laws. I am determined that I will have everlasting life in the kingdom with Our Father and Jesus!

No, it was not easy at first for me to live according to the principle of God. In fact, I fell many, many times trying to get it right! The thought (planted in my mind by the Devil) of not enjoying life and having fun anymore I just could not bear. Oh, I wanted to enjoy life to the fullest. I did not want to live, what I thought would be a mundane life! Again, this is what the Devil had me believing. I am here to tell you that this is another lie of Satan! Life with Christ is full of excitement and a peace that surpasses all understanding! I am telling you it is "Awesome!"

Getting back on track here, one morning I had just hung up the telephone after talking to my husband and he said that he would call me back after we talk and I hung up the telephone. A few minutes later I pick the phone up to call my sister in law, and the telephone service had trouble on the line I could not get through. This frustrated me. Then the cable went out, I can't watch the Inspiration Channel! Oh, I am in a tizzy now, I cannot hear the word of God today for strength! I cannot watch Joyce Meyers ministry! Okay now I am really getting frustrated. Bam, it hit me! Okay, this is the Devil at work again messing with my head. I confess yes, for a brief moment I was worrying, fearful and angry.

But, I began to talk to Jesus about this situation and then the Holy Spirit announced to me what was happening. He gave to me discernment and understanding. Then I began to realize that this was a test. My sincerity in giving my life to Christ was being tested! Well, I passed this test! I passed the test because of my love, devotion, determination and the Spirit of God! I was tested with the things of the world, that I had become attached to and felt that I needed.

I thank God for giving me this new life and filling me His Holy Spirit. I thank God that it is His Spirit the lives in me that gives me discernment and understanding. I acknowledged and realized that the Devil was trying to mentally torment me. But I received the victory through Christ Jesus.

I realized that I did not need a telephone to communicate with my husband. I could go next door and use the neighbors phone! And I did! I did not need cable for Spiritual Strength. I have the Word of

Acknowledge, Beware and Recognize

God that He will strengthen and keep me! And He did. I have the word of God that He will never leave me or forsake me. And He didn't. He said that He would send to me a comforter, the Holy Spirit! And He did! I also have the "BIBLE" and I can read! And I did! All Praise to God!

Yeah, Satan seized the opportunity and use this situation to attack me. I also realized that I was being tested. I realized that I could really give up the luxury, the things of the world for God, without feeling regret or frustrated? Well Satan and I surely bumped heads, because I am as determined to have peace, as he is to torment me, I had the victory! I realized that I don't need a telephone, if I need to make a call there is the neighbors phone or the pay phone. As for cable TV and Insp, I have a bible and I can read.

I thank God that I am here today alive, drug free, healed and blessed. And I am strong because He loves me! I know that God has kept me in existence because He loves me and also for the sake of Him showing His power and in order to have His name declared in all the earth! Exodus 9:16

I am very determined to live my life for God, to serve Him, to please Him and to be a blessing to others. Yes! I am telling you that I have something in common with the Devil!

'DETERMINATION' The Devil is determined to destroy and kill me. I am determined that he is not! I am "DETERMINED" to follow Jesus and be like Jesus! See what Jesus has done for me!

"BE DETERMINED, SATAN IS!"

Audrey F. Evans-Ford

You Are Never Alone!

I believe that mans greatest fear is being alone. I know that it was my greatest fear. I never wanted to be alone or by myself. The thought of being alone frightened me. Everyone wants someone so that they will not be alone. Yes, "Every one" even those who say that they don't need anyone. In fact the next time someone tells you that, tell them to tell that to God!

It is written in Genesis 2:18-22 that God said that is not good for the man to be alone. And this is why God formed from the ground every wild beast of the field and every flying creature of the heavens and brought them to Adam, so that Adam would not be alone. But God saw that Adam was still alone. So, God had a deep sleep fall upon Adam and while he was sleeping, God took one of Adams ribs and proceeded to make him a woman, to complement him and be a help for him.

What does this tell you? God said that it is not good for man to be alone. God meant that! Many of us become afraid when we think that we are alone and have no one. It is natural for us to feel this way because God created us and filled us with the desire for companionship. And no, no one wants to be alone.

Many of us need to obtain an accurate knowledge of Gods word and become obedient to His laws and principles and see what God does for us all. Believe me you are never alone. Have you ever really thought about just how much Jesus loves us? Just think about it, even after being hung and nailed to the cross, Jesus still asked our Father to forgive us. And Jesus also kept His promise to us! He asked our Father to send to us a comforter and a helper so that we would never be alone!

Even though the Comforter has been sent to us, we sometimes still feel alone. I know that I do at times. Let me tell you what I have discovered about feeling that I am alone. It is during these times that I need to focus on God! And still yet, sometimes my heart will still long for someone to talk to. But, when I know that it is not about to happen, I just pray and I ask Jesus to strengthen me and help me through my times of loneliness. And believe it or not He helps me and comforts me. And He says to me; Audrey it is okay.

Acknowledge, Beware and Recognize

Most of my days during this particular time in my life appear to be boring, mundane and not very exciting. I am alone for the most part as for as companionship of another human being. And I know that it is because I have surrendered my life to Jesus. This time that I spend alone away from human companions is my time to grow and become closer and more intimate with God. During this time I am not really alone, I am spending this time with God and being prepared Spiritually, Mentally, Emotionally and Physically for my future in Christ and the things that are to come. I acknowledge that I am not alone at all!

At times when I realize that I am beginning to feel alone, I snap out of it quickly! Because I know that the Devil will try to tempt me to do something stupid so that I won't be alone. I thank God for filling me with His Spirit. His Spirit lead and direct me in the way that I should go in all affairs of my life. He really does help me. I no longer think like I use to think. I don't feel like I use to feel. I don't hang out in the places that I use to. I don't want to, I have no desire to. And yes, even now, I still sometimes have a moment or two when I feel alone.

But, I have made my decision and I am determined to stick with it! I made my choice and decided that I am going to live according to the laws and principles of God! This means giving up my sinful ways, my sinful life! And a lot of old associates! I am determined to do this at whatever cost! Yes, there are times when I really feel so alone. Remember the title of this book; "Acknowledge, Beware and Recognize" Okay! Watch out for our adversary "Satan!" You see, during our periods of loneliness we are vulnerable and these are times of weakness and Satan is all over us, like white on rice trying to tempt us to seek companionship and the wrong kind!

Satan will suffocate you to the point that you will probably begin to hyperventilate from his nagging, trying to tempt you to do the very things that you no longer want to do. Satan tries to tempt you to be with people that he knows you need not hang with. Oh, I am not telling you to be unkind or unloving to anyone because no one can make you do anything that you don't want to do. But they can be used as tools of Satan to tempt you to do wrong. You know what is best for you.

I thank God that when Satan approaches me in my moments of weakness, that His Spirit announces to me, that the adversary is on the prowl. Then I remember what hurt and destruction that Satan has already caused in my life. I don't want it anymore. Therefore, I refuse to listen to the lies of Satan.

For example, when I would feel lonely I go and sit out on my sons' back porch. I begin to pray and talk to God. And do you know that the Devil will just come and butt in my conversation with God like he was invited! I have to tell you the Devil is really something. He begins to try to penetrate my mind with negative thoughts. He tries to tempt me to go hang out with those that he know that I have given up hanging out with for the soul purpose of being obedient to God and staying clean!

So when Satan does this, I just simply continue talking and praying to God. Then the Spirit of God asks me; Audrey if you could go anywhere today, where would you go? Who do you want to see? Do you want to be with your husband today? If you were with your husband today, what would you be doing? After asking these questions, I realize that there was no place that I want to go. There was no one that I want to see. And I did not want to be with my husband at this time either. I would rather be alone with Jesus. I know that when the time is right, He will bring me in the presence of others that has been called into union with Him and our Father. Yes, He will give to me new friends! Amen

The problem with most of us is that we are accustomed to the touch of the flesh and not the presence of the Holy Spirit! We have a need for human companionship! This is okay, because God made woman so that man would not be alone. And for those of us who do not have some one in our lives for human companionship, we need to know that we are still not alone. We are not alone because Jesus sent to us some one special, so that we will not ever be alone, He sent to us His Spirit that lives in us!

If you are obedient to the laws and principles of God you will know that He is with you. Jesus said in John 14: 12-17 that if we love Him and observe His commandments; that He will request the Father and He will give us another helper to be with us forever, the spirit of the truth **"which the world cannot receive"**, but we can. You (we) will know the spirit because it remains with you (us) and is in you (us). Jesus said that He will not leave or forsaken us!

Satan uses your loneliness as a weapon to convince you that you have no one and that no one loves you or cares about you. Satan is a liar! Jesus loves you and He cares about you. And if you ask Him for a companion, He will give you one! Ask Him!

You are never alone, Jesus said, "**I WILL BY NO MEANS LEAVE YOU NOR BY ANY MEANS FORSAKE YOU!**" (Hebrew 13:5-6)

*********YOU ARE NEVER ALONE!********

Audrey F. Evans-Ford

JEREMIAH CHAPTER 45

(Edited)

ORDER IT! Order the buckler and shield because you are drawn near to battle. Harness the horses and mount up! Stand forth with your helmets. Polish your spears and put on the complete Armour of God!

Do not fear and do not be dismayed. God will save you and your offspring from afar. You shall return from the battle and have rest and be at ease. No one shall make you afraid!

Do not fear for you are a servant of God. God is with you and He will make a complete end to your enemies and He will not make a complete end of you!

God will lead you, He will guide you, He will protect you and He will correct you!

God will never leave you nor fail you! Praise God!

Application of Strength

Do not be impatient with God! When you find yourself becoming impatient waiting for God. Catch yourself and Stop! Stop focusing on yourself and your problems. Focus on God. Take time and think about God. Think about what God has already done for you. Is this hard for you to do? Okay then try to remember the most painful and distressing time in your life. Think about how you wanted to just give up and probably at times wanted to die and wondered why you were even alive? Think about those horrible times. Seriously, "Pause" and think about them!

Can you really remember the agony, the pain and the suffering? It is kind of hard to do now is'nt it, now that the pain is gone. I wonder why? Could it be because God as always brought us through those bad times leaving us with no pain to remember? Sure we can remember the bad situation and hard times in life. At times we reminisce and talk about those times, we talk about the pain, but we do not actually feel the pain that we had. It is gone!

Like breaking an arm or a leg. The pain of the break is excruciating, it is unbearable and you just can't take it anymore. HELP! Help me somebody! Please, I can't take it! Sounds familiar. The doctor applies an anesthetic and the pain is gone. Later you have thoughts about what the pain was like. But you really can't remember the pain because it is gone! You really try to remember the pain, but you can't, you can't because you can't feel it. Even when you try to focus in on the pain that you know was there, you can't, because it is gone. This is true about all pain rather it is physical, mental or emotional. Who brought you through your pain? Could it possibly have been God?

Well I boldly and loudly announce that it is God my Father that bought me through all my trials, tribulations and pain. Who or what brought you through yours? Was it God? Okay so you are going through something again, and? Stop and praise God! Thank God for all that He has already done for you! Thank God for taking away your pain in the past and trust Him to do it again! Thank God for what He is now doing for you.

What is hurting you and giving you pain now? Oh, you have asked God for something and He is not answering your prayer fast enough. You are distressed, frustrated and even aggravated. You want your prayer answered right now! Well, in case you do not know it, let me be the first to tell you that it does not work like that! How long did it take for you to become obedient to His word, better yet, are you being obedient to His word now? Think about it! God is always giving to you, what do you give to Him, other than your problems.

Yeah, I know that there is someone right now that is probably saying, "God has not always answered my prayers." Wrong! Yes He did. You just did not acknowledge that He did. I know this, because I have said the same thing to myself many times. Guess what? I was wrong. God did answer my prayers but I was being disobedient to His word doing things my way and being impatient. I blew it! I blew my answered prayer because I interfered with Gods work and manipulated the situation because I was impatient waiting on God! Or because I was impatient, I gave up praying for what I wanted and said later for it, I don't want it anyway, or it is not worth waiting for. Many times I did not want the agony of waiting. So I gave up and did not wait for God to answer my prayer! But, I have since learned that anything that is not worth waiting for is not worth praying for!

God always answer our prayers. Are you sincere and obedient to Gods' laws? Are you living according to Gods' principles? We must stop doing things our way and trust God. God does not need our help or interference. God does not need anything from us. We need God. We need to be sincere and obedient to His word. We need to trust and have faith in Him. Once we have asked God for anything, trust Him to give it to us. Stand on His word having faith that His word will not return void.

God loves us and Jesus assures us in Isaiah 55:11 that His word that goes forth from His mouth shall not return to Him void, but His word will prove to be!" Jesus also tells us in Matthew 7:7-8 to keep on asking and it will be given to you; keep seeking and you shall find; keep on knocking and it will be opened to you. Everyone asking receives! Gods' word is unchangeable! He means what He says, ask for anything and you shall receive it! Stop being impatient! God already has answered your prayer! If for no other reason than to show you His power, your prayer is answered!

Acknowledge, Beware and Recognize

God honors His word! If God said He will do! Ask and it is done! No, we don't know how He will do it, or when He will do it. But, know that He will do it **in His time**! Your application of strength is in the word of God! Apply it when Satan attacks you with negative thoughts causing you to doubt God! Remember Satan is a liar and a great deceiver!

Remember! God is in control of every life, yours, mine and theirs. God is in control of every situation and circumstance. So, stop complaining! Praise God for His love and faithfulness. Give Him praise sometimes instead of your problems all the time. Apply the word of God to your life everyday and be obedient to it! Go on! Rejoice knowing that God loves you and that He always do what He says He will do! Stay focused on God and not the problem! He has already handled it! Don't you know!

"GODS WORD IS APPLICATION FOR STRENGTH!"

Audrey F. Evans-Ford

Psalm 27 (Revised)

The Lord Jesus is my light and my salvation. Who shall I fear?
Jesus is the strength of my life. In this my heart is confident! My heart shall not fear!
One thing I have desire of my Lord Jesus that I will seek: That I may dwell in His house all the days of my life. To behold the beauty of the Lord Jesus, the Lamb of God!
In my times of trouble I request of you Lord Jesus to hide me and set me high upon a rock and lift my head up above all my enemies that are around and about me.
Lord Jesus you have been my help and you did not leave or forsake me. When those that I love forsaken me, Lord Jesus you were there for me and cared for me!
Lord Jesus please continue to teach me your ways and lead me in a smooth path and delivered me from the will of my adversaries. I would have lost heart if it had not been for you my Lord, my God!
It is your goodness Lord Jesus that I see living in the land. It is your mercy and grace that gave me courage and strength! I Have Faith! And I wait Lord Jesus for you to act! I just pray and wait!

Acknowledge, Beware and Recognize

DO YOU WANT A BETTER LIFE?

Do You Really Know God?

I am not asking you have you heard of God. My question is "Do you know God?" You see many of us have heard of God, but we do not "Know God"!

We have been told, taught and have even read about God, and yet we still do not know Him. Have you ever thought about it? Have you ever asked yourself do you really know God? Have you ever had the desire or have the desire to really know God?

Guess what? God wants you to know Him! God loves you. He is your Father. We are all His children and this means you too! God wants you to know Him and to know just how much He loves you!

Many of us have been taught that we are sinners, we are bad and God our Father is angry with us for sinning. Knowing that we are sinners and that God is our Father, we have much fear of Him because of our sins and we focus on the sin instead of Gods love for us. Sure, we are also taught that God forgives us for our sins, but with most of us we do not realize that it is Gods love for us, that our sins are forgiven. We do not really know Gods love.

Let me tell you a little about myself. I grew up in a home of alcohol, mental, physical and verbal abuse that eventually became a broken home. I was brought up in church until I was twelve. From that point on I grew up confused and rebelling, I did not know who I was or what I was. I had been told many times that I should have been flushed. Then to top that I was a member of a church that taught me to pray and say to my Father God, that I am unworthy! How could I after growing up in this type of environment and believe that God would forgive me or even yet, how could I believe that God loved me? I was nothing, a nobody and unworthy. I really believed this. Why? Because I was a sinner and I did not know God!

I Thank God for His love. I was told about Gods love and I read about His love, but no one ever really told me just how much God loves me. I did not have a personal relationship with God, so I did not personally know His love for me. Now that I have surrendered my life to God I realize how much He really does love me.

I have also learned that we must love our Father God with our entire being. We should become intimate with Him and draw closer to Him. It is written in the book of Matthew 22:37 that, "We must Love God our Father with our whole hearts, with all our souls, and with all our minds!" It is so sad that there is not enough emphasis put in **teaching** us to First, **Love God** above all things! I am a witness that if you start showing God just a little love that He will show you a lot of Love! There is no one that can express or show you Gods love better than God Himself!

We are always being taught to surrender our lives to Christ and repent. For some reason the word "repent" seems to mean go on and get your punishment. Well let me put it to you like this, I use to think the word repent meant to go on and take your punishment and get it over! Many of us want to surrender, but we are afraid to because we are thinking about being punished rather than being forgiven for our sins. We feel that our sin is the worst and that the punishment will be greater. Second we are afraid because we think that to surrender our lives to God means that we will not enjoy life any more. Third we believe that to surrender our lives to Christ means sacrifice and the word 'sacrifice' itself is frightening.

Fear is a weapon of Satan. All these fears that we have are of the Devil. Satan wants you to believe this pack of lies. Why? To keep you from your rightful inheritance and the Kingdom of Heaven! Satan wants your soul and your company in hell with him, where he is the Host! He offers you his glass of a living death, pain, suffering and eternal torment!

I am here to tell you that Satan is a "LIAR!" Obey the First law of our Father God! Become intimate with Him, loving Him with your entire being, your heart, your soul and your mind. Watch what happens in your life. Watch God pour out His blessings!

It is like this, when you start loving God with your entire being and becoming intimate, getting closer and closer to Him, Guess What? No one will have to tell you or suggest to you to surrender your life to Him. You will lovingly and willingly surrender it to Him!

There is a big difference in you willingly surrendering your life to Christ and having some one to tell you to do it. If you are anything like I use to be, you really do not want anyone telling you what to do

Acknowledge, Beware and Recognize

at all and you will rebel. My attitude was "How can you tell me to repent when you are a sinner yourself!" Boy, I sure thank God for renewing my mind! Thank you Jesus!

As you become closer to God the fears that you have about surrendering your life to Him will no longer exist. You will know that God's love for you is greater than any sin that you could ever commit! You will know that Our Father God truly loves you and forgives you. He does not punish you. Sure, He disciplines you and He does this because He loves you! Think about it this way, who would you rather have discipline you, our Father God or Satan our Enemy?

So, you think that surrendering your life to Christ means no more fun, life will be boring, no more excitement! This is not so, it's a lie of Satan! You will be in total awe with your new life in Christ, not only will it be exciting, it will be more exciting then you can ever begin to imagine. I am telling you it is "AWESOME!" God forgives and blesses His children. This is why you are reading this book! Because God forgave me and blessed me!

You also think that you have to make sacrifices. You have to give up the things that you treasure, love and like! Just what are your treasures? What is it that you will be sacrificing? Well, let me put it to you like this, "God Gave His Only Begotten Son, Jesus" for you, then **Jesus gave His Life for you**! Jesus gave His life as a 'one time' sacrifice for all of us! Now ask yourself, **"What greater sacrifice could you give for Him?"** Think about it! You are not being asked to sacrifice anything! Jesus life was the perfect and only sacrifice needed.

Think about how God has shown you His love! Before His Son Jesus came into the world, God made a covenant with us through His Word! We still defied Him and what did God do? He sent His Son, Jesus Christ into the world to live among us sinners, forgiving us, loving us and still blessing us! What kind of love is this? Is this not a love that surpasses all of mankind understanding?

God's love for us is beyond our understanding. Isn't it wonderful that He loves us as He does? Why is it so difficult for us to love Him? Why can't we be grateful, thankful and faithful to Him? Why? Why is it so hard for us to give up the things of the world and Love Him with our entire being and be obedient to His word and live according to His principles? Why do we continue to let Satan have his way in our lives? We know that Satan has nothing but hate for us and he wants to destroy and kill us!

Our Father God loves us with all our sins and flaws! He has given us life, His Word, His Son, His Angels and a free will. And Our Father God does not force us to love Him or surrender our lives to Him. Instead, He waits for us to make our choice.

My original question is "Do You Really Know God?" Do you? If you do not really know God, do not be alarmed and do not be afraid to admit it. God already know what you know and what you don't know. He loves you just the same. If you have the desire to know God, all you need to do is love Him! Spend time with Him and become intimate with Him. Draw close to Him. Diligently seek Him and see His love and wonderful works performed in your life!

Listen, out of all the things that you have learned, read and have been taught about our Father, the most important things to know is that, all **Our Father is asking** of **us**, "**is for us to Love Him**!" and "To Love Him **with our entire being**!" Putting nothing and no one before Him! **That's All**! What is so complicated about loving our Father with our entire being? We love our husbands, wives, children, parents, other family member, friends etc… Don't you know that it is because of God our Father that they exist!

Brothers and Sisters, we all have to make our choice and we truly need to make it, like in yesterday! I just want you to know that I made my choice. I have chosen my life in Christ. And my life is not mundane at all. On the contrary my life is exciting and I am continually being abundantly blessed!

It is imperative that you make a "DECISION" and it is in your best interest to do it now! Because it is written in Acts 1:7 that Jesus Said, "It does not belong to you to get knowledge of the times and seasons, which the Father has placed in His own jurisdiction!" Meaning no one, not even Jesus Christ Himself knows the day of "Judgment" or when He will return!

If you find it difficult deciding rather or not to surrender your life to Christ, because you don't know who you are, are what you are and you do not know what you want, ask yourself these questions;
1. Do I believe in God?
2. Do I believe that Jesus Christ is the Son of God and my Savior?
3. Do I want a life of joy, peace, happiness, and riches?

Acknowledge, Beware and Recognize

If your answer is yes to any of these questions than, draw closer to Our Father and become intimate with Him. Also know that you have been made the righteousness of Our Father God through the shed blood of Jesus Christ! Don't be deceived by Satan lies any longer! Don't be afraid! Make your Decision and receive your inheritance, now!

"LOVE YOUR FATHER GOD WITH ALL YOUR HEART!"

Audrey F. Evans-Ford

Psalm 85

Lord you have been favorable to your land; You have brought back the captivity of Jacob. You have forgiven the iniquity of your people; You have covered their sins. You have taken away all your wrath; You have turned from the fierceness of you anger.

Restore us, O God of our salvation and cause your anger toward us to cease. Will you be anger with us forever? Will you prolong your anger to all generations? Will you not revive us again, that your people may rejoice in you? Show us your mercy Lord and grant us your salvation.

I will hear what God the Lord will speak, For He will speak peace to His people and to His saints; But let them not turn back to folly. Surely His salvation is near to those who fear Him. That glory may dwell in our land.

Mercy and truth have met together; Righteousness and peace have kissed. Truth shall spring out of the earth, and righteousness shall look down from heaven.

Yes, the Lord will give what is good; and our land will yield its increase. Righteousness will go before Him and shall make His footsteps our pathway.

The Decision!

Are you thinking about surrendering your life to Jesus Christ? Well before answering this question, first ask yourself: "Do You Love Jesus The Way That He Loves You?"
1. Would you give your life for Jesus?
2. Do you want to be like Jesus?
3. Are you willing to be obedient to the word of God?
4. Are you willing to live according to the principles of God?
5. Do you know that surrendering your life to Christ means giving up your life in the world?
6. Do you know that giving up your life in the world means to trust God to supply all your needs and desires?
7. Do you know that giving up your life in the world and giving up the worldly things means that you are breaking free from the bondage of sin and death and resisting Satan?

Then you need to know that Satan is very angry with you if you have made the decision to give your life to Christ!

Resisting Satan and becoming obedient to Gods laws, means that you are no longer doing what Satan wants you to do. Therefore, Satan is very angry with you and he is even more determined to kill you! And Satan is not going to let go without a fight! He wants to keep you!

Now here are some more questions for you:
1. Are you ready to surrender your life to Jesus?
2. Are you ready to commit your life to Jesus?
3. Are you willing to fight for you right to a new life?
4. Are you ready to resist Satan?
5. Are you afraid of Satan?
6. Are you worried, nervous and maybe a little unsure about surrendering your life to Christ ?
7. Do you believe that God is the creator of all things that exist? Including Satan!
8. Do you believe that Jesus Christ really love you?
9. Do you believe that Jesus died and defeated Satan for you?
10. Do you know that Jesus has All Authority over Satan?

11. Do you "TRUST" God and Our Savior Jesus Christ?
12. Do you know that Jesus sent to you a comforter?
13. Do you know that God and Jesus Christ is the Holy Spirit?

Then know that if you have decided to give your life to Christ that there is nothing to fear. God has sent His Holy Spirit our comforter to guide and protect those of us who have surrendered our lives to Him. And those of us that diligently seek His kingdom and His righteousness shall not only be blessed, but protected too!

Do not be afraid of Satan or afraid to surrender your life to God. Surrender your life totally and completely to God. Satan cannot harm nor hurt you. His does not have the power!

Let me tell you something, it is written in Isaiah 40:29 that God gives to His weak ones strength and He gives power to the tired ones; and He gives to the ones without dynamic energy His full might abound. We are told in 2 Corinthians that, "Our weapons of our warfare is not of the flesh, but of the spirits of darkness and God is **powerfully** overturning strongly entrenched things!

Let me assure you and it is written in 2 Timothy 1:7 that, "Our Father gives to His children that diligently seek Him, His spirit that is of power, love, peace and a sound mind." And through Jesus our Father has given us His Holy Spirit. Therefore, we have inherited our Fathers power and we have the Authority over all the power of the enemy, our adversary, Satan!

Remember the Devil brings us death! But, Jesus conquered death, so that we might have eternal life in the Kingdom of Heaven!

PSALM 86

Bow down your ear and Lord hear me. I am poor and needy.
Preserve my life, for you are my God. Save me your servant who trusts in you! Be merciful to me, O Lord, I cry to you all day long. Rejoice the soul of your servant, to you O Lord I lift up my soul. For you Lord are good and ready to forgive. And abundant in mercy to all those who call upon you!
Give ear, O Lord to my prayer and attend to the voice of my supplications. In the day of my trouble I will call upon you. For you will answer me. You O Lord are mighty and powerful and there are no works like yours.
All nations whom you have made shall come and worship before you, O Lord and shall glorify your name. For you are great and do wondrous things. You alone are God! Teach me your way, O Lord; I will walk in your truth; Unite my heart to fear your name. I will praise you, O Lord my God, with all my heart. And I will glorify your name forever more. For great is your mercy toward me, and you have delivered my soul from the depths of Hell!
O God the proud have risen against me and a mob of violent men have sought my life and have not set you before them. But you, O Lord are a God full of compassion and gracious, longsuffering and abundant in mercy and truth.
Oh, turn to me, and have mercy on me! Give your strength to your servant and save the son of your maidservant. Show me a sign for good, so that those who hate me may see it and be a shame. Because you, Lord, have helped me and comforted me!
Thank you My Lord, My God!

Audrey F. Evans-Ford

I Am Not Really A Sinner!

Have you ever said or ever heard someone else say; "I am not really a sinner!" I have. But, in reference to myself, I knew that I was a sinner and it is not that I wanted to be nor was it my choice. I was born into sin. It is even written in the book of Psalms 51:5 that, "I was brought forth with birth pains and in sin my mother conceived me!" And guess what? So were you!

I realize that most people see sinners as people that use profanity, rob, steal, kill and abuse drugs and alcohol. And many people that do not do these things feel as though they are righteous and without sin. **WRONG**! Satan has blind them, big time! They too are sinners. And this is written in Romans 3:10 that, "There is not a righteous man, not even one." This means not even you or I!

Do you know what sin is? Sin is all things that oppose the word of God. Sin is breaking the laws of God. And sinners are those of us that are breaking Gods laws and not living according to His principles. Sin is choosing to do wrong instead of doing right! Sin is defiling our bodies with anything that brings it harm! Rather it is drugs, alcohol, food, cigarettes, or whatever. (Our body is the temple for the Holy Spirit, the spirit of God Himself!) Sin is arrogance, lies, blasphemy, gossip, greed, selfishness, hate, lust, deception, fornication, adultery and being judgmental of others! It is written in 1 John 5:17 that, "All unrighteousness is sin"

For those of you, who feel that you are not 'really' a sinner, I strongly suggest that you re-evaluate yourself. If you think or even feel this way then you have committed a sin. You are calling God a liar! Read it in Romans 3:23 that, "For all have sinned (yes, even you) and fallen short of the glory of God." And this is why God sent Jesus into the world, "as an offering for propitiation through faith in His blood" so that we may be saved from our sins!

Yes, we are all sinners. And we are also Gods children and our sins are forgiven for His name sake! Our Father knows what we are up against! He knows Satan and his works! Our Father knows that in these lasts days that hard times are critical for us to deal with.

It is written in 2 Timothy that we are **not** to **be lovers of ourselves** and **of money**. We are told **not** to **be self-assuming, haughty, blasphemers** nor **disobedient to parents**. We are **not to be unthankful, disloyal**, having no natural affection. We are **not to be slanderers** and **without self-control**. We are **not** to **be fierce, without love** of **goodness, betrayers, headstrong** and **puffed up with pride**. We are **not to be lovers of pleasures rather than lovers of God**. Nor have a form of godly devotion but proving false to its power. **We must turn away from these things!**

These things arouse men who slyly work their way into households and lead as they captive weak women loaded down with sins and led by various desires. They are always learning and yet they never are able to come to an accurate knowledge of "Truth." We are told in 2Timothy 3:1-7 to, "Be strong, turn away from these things."

Jesus told us to, "Keep your senses, be watchful. Our Adversary, the Devil walks about like a roaring lion, seeking to devour [you]!" And this is written in 1Peter 5:8. We are not to be lovers of either the world or the things in the world. If we are a lover of the world, then the love of our Father is not in us. You see, everything in the world desires the flesh and the eyes. To show and display one's means of life and it does not originate from '**God**' it originates with the world and from Satan!

Am I really a sinner? Are you really a sinner? We all are sinners, and there is no such thing as a big sin or a little sin, a sin is a sin and a sinner is a sinner! Thank God that He sent His son Jesus to purchase our souls. Jesus redeemed us by shedding His blood! It is written in 1 John 4:4 that we originate with our Father and sin has been conquered because it is God that is in union with us that is greater than he (Satan) that is in this world! Therefore, let us be imitators of Christ Jesus and do what is good because we originate from our Father! Let us build ourselves on Holy faith praying and keeping ourselves in God's love, while we wait for the mercy of our Lord Jesus Christ with eternal life in view!

There is no such thing as a "not really a sinner" we are all sinners. Isn't it awesome that even though we are sinners, we belong to our Father God and He forgives us for our sins! It is written in Hebrew 8:10-12 that Our Father said that He will become our God and we will be His children. He will put His laws in our mind and hearts and no one will have to teach us to know Him, because we will already know

Him, each and every last one of us. God said He will be merciful to our unrighteous deeds and by no means will He call our sins to mind anymore.

Now, knowing that we are all sinners, we also know that we have to make a choice as to where we want to spend the rest of our eternal lives. There are only two places, **Heaven or Hell**? Need I say more?

I Thank God for Being My Father, What About You?

Have You Made Your Decision?

Well, have you made your decision? If you have, then remember **the First commandment** of God our Father, which is written in Matthew 22:37 **"Thou Shalt Love The Lord Thy God With All Thy Heart and With All Thy Soul and All Thy Mind!"**

It is very important that you Love Our Father God with your entire being. Seek His kingdom and His righteousness and know that all other things shall be added to your life. Also keep your minds fixed on the things above and not on the things on this earth.

Now, if you have committed your life to Christ, then know that you are in union with Christ and Our Father God. And whatever you are doing, be sure that you are doing it for the glory of God. We are told in 1 Corinthians 10:31-32 to "Do all things for the glory of God, so that you and the congregation of Gods people do not stumble and fall."

To do this you must not just believe, but you must know that God is your Father and creator. You see, believing is not enough because most of us only believe in what we see and it is hard for many of us to believe in the unseen. You must know in your mind as you know it in your heart that God is our Father and Jesus Christ is His Son our Savior.

For example, you know your name. No matter what the situation or circumstance may be, you know your name. You can even change your name, and yet you will still remember and know what your given name was. Well, this is how you should know God. Know that God is our Father, like you know your name!

Become intimate with God and give Him first place in your life. Become intimate with God so that you will know His will. Seek and learn His will and you'll make your daily schedule around God and do only the things that you know He would have you to do. Be obedient to His Holy Spirit that lives in you. The Holy Spirit will lead and guide you in all that you do. Being obedient to the Holy Spirit will keep you from carrying out fleshy desires.

It is even written in Galatians 5:17 that the desires of the flesh is against Gods' Holy Spirit and the Holy Spirit is against the flesh, therefore the things that your flesh would have you to do, you will not do! You need to know that you are not wrestling with flesh and blood. But, you are wrestling against the world rulers of darkness and the spiritual wickedness in heavenly places. And if you have surrendered your life to Jesus, then you are in heavenly places!

Remember and acknowledge that Satan is determined to destroy and kill you and he is not letting go of you without a fight! Are you ready? Look, don't worry about what other people say or think about you. Do not be a shame to live a righteous life with Jesus! It is written in John 15 that the world hated Jesus and crucified Him before they hated you. And remember Jesus is coming back for His righteous ones!

Each day, take about maybe fifteen to thirty minutes and read the Book of John in your Bible and read the word of God and His promises made to you, and know that Our Father God and His Son Jesus Christ is not a "LIAR!" Gods' word will not return to Him void. God watches over His word to perform it. In fact our Father magnifies His word above His name!

In the Book of John chapters 14 and 15, Jesus says that those of us who keep His commandments and observes them, we are the ones that love Him. And those of us that love Him will be loved by His Father (Our Father God) and He will love us and He will plainly show Himself to us!" and "If anyone loves Him, we will observe His word and His Father (Our Father) will love us and we shall come to Him and make our abode with Him. Jesus says if we remain in union with Him that His sayings will remain in us, and that for us to ask whatever we wish and it will take place for us.

I am informing you of all these things so that you will not have to worry or be unsure as to whether or not you want to surrender your life to God. Jesus said that He shall never leave or forsaken you and He won't! But, the decision for you to surrender your life to Him is yours and yours alone! God wants you to become intimate with Him and give Him first place in your life.

Satan is going to do all that he can to stop you from surrendering your life to God! He is going to place doubt in your mind as to whether or not Gods' word is true. Satan is going to make you unsure about your decision. It is Satan's job to stop you. Don't let him. For the sake of your soul, please, don't let Satan stop you from surrendering your life to God!

Acknowledge, Beware and Recognize

It is imperative that you become very intimate with God so that you will know His will for your life as well as His word. Don't worry about Satan or anything!

God wants me to remind you of the Book of John and what Jesus said:

Jesus said, "He that has my commandments and observes them, that one is he who loves me. In turn he that loves me will be loved by my Father and I will love him and I will plainly show myself to him." (14:21)

"If anyone loves me, he will observe my word and my Father will love him and we shall come to him and make our abode with him." (14:23)

"Jesus said that when He ascends into Heaven His Father would send to us a helper, the Holy Spirit and the Holy Spirit will teach us all things and bring back to our minds all things that He has told us." (14:26)

Jesus said, "I leave you peace, I give you my peace. I do not give it to you the way that the world gives it. Do not let your heart be troubled nor let them shrink for fear."

"If you remain in union with me and my sayings remain in you, ask whatever you will and it will take place for you." (15:7)

"I am the vine you are the branches. He that remains in union with me and I in union with him, this one bears much fruit because apart from me you can do nothing at all!" (15:5)

Jesus says that, "If the world hates you, (don't be troubled) you know that it (the world) has hated me (him) before it hated you." (15:17)

Don't worry about what other people say or think about you. Do not be a shame to live the life of righteousness with Jesus Christ! Remember Jesus is coming back for His righteous ones, He said it and He will do it, Jesus is coming back! Jesus said, "I am going away and I am coming back to you!" (14:28)

You are no longer a stranger or alien to God, but you are fellow citizens of the holy ones and are members of the household of God. You are in union with God and you too, are being built up together into a place for God to inhabit by spirit! (Ephesians 2:19,22)

So, be careful and do not be mislead. Return to God and take your commitment to Jesus seriously! Get out of the world of sin and into the Word of God and be what you were created to be, His righteous one!

We are Gods children and we need to, as it is written in 1 Corinthians 16:13 "Stay awake and stand firm in faith and carry on as (children of God) men and grow mighty. And "Clothe ourselves with love for love is the perfect bond of union with Christ Jesus and this is written in Colossians 3:14.

"THE DECISION IS YOURS, AND YOURS ALONE!"

Psalm 21 Revised

"Joy in the Salvation of the Lord"

I shall have joy in your strength, O Lord; And in Your salvation how greatly shall I rejoice! You have given me my heart's desire, and have not withheld the request of my lips.

You meet me with the blessings of goodness; I asked life from You and You gave it to me. You have lengthen my days. My glory is great in Your salvation; Honor and majesty You have placed upon me.

You have made me most blessed forever; You have made me exceedingly glad with Your presence. I trust in You O Lord, and through the mercy of the Most High I shall not be moved.

Your hand will find all my enemies; Your right hand will find those who hate me. You shall make them as a fiery oven in the time of Your anger, Lord you shall swallow them up in Your wrath, and the fire shall devour them.

They intended evil against me; they devised a plot which they are not able to perform. Therefore You will make them turn their back; You will make ready Your arrows on Your string toward their faces.

Be exalted, O Lord my God, in Your Own Strength! I will sing and praise Your Powers, forever!

Audrey F. Evans-Ford

Two Years of Stumbling

It has taken me two years of stumbling and falling to complete this book. Why?

It was in 1999 that I finally realized that God was truly calling me to serve Him and writing is one of the ways that He has called me to serve Him. I did not feel that my life was worth living and there was just no way that God would use me for anything. I was stuck on stupid, weak and a drug user. I felt totally unworthy! I Thank God for not giving up on me even when I wandered away from Him!

I realize that Gods love for me is forever, no matter what. He has given me His grace and mercy and has shown me favor! It has taken me two years to write this book because I kept stumbling and falling back into the world and out of His word!

I was really sincere about doing the will of God and staying away from worldly things. Guess what? Satan was sincere too! Satan was determined that he was not going to let go of me and let God have me! I did not know that then, but I know it now. This is why I thank God for His love!

I was diligently seeking the wisdom and knowledge of God and trying to be obedient to His laws and live according to His principles. It was rough for a while. I was struggling to do Gods will and Satan kept pulling me his way. I had stopped smoking crack, cursing, stealing, smoking cigarettes and drinking alcohol. I had even started fasting. Then "BAM!" out of nowhere, I would fall again! And God would be there every time I would fall and He picked me up! Again, and again and again! Yes, My God is an awesome God!

In February, 2001 a voice spoke to me every night for two weeks telling me to get baptized. The voice even told me who was to baptize me. So, I obeyed the voice that spoke to me and on March 30, 2001, I was baptized! After the baptism the minister that baptized me said to me, "The Devil is going to be all over you" and for me to watch out for him! Well, the Pastor was right! Satan attacked me like some folk would say, "Like forty going north!" and I backslid.

I tell you, I felt like a boulder rolling down a mountain. But, God because of His love and compassion for me showed me that I was not

Acknowledge, Beware and Recognize

falling, I was just stumbling! I had just been born again in Christ, and therefore, I was a baby, trying to walk, but stumbling. God assured me that as I get to know Him and obtain wisdom and knowledge that I will grow and become stronger. And I would not continue to stumble and fall!

Well during all my stumbling and falling, I started back using drugs. I lost my husband and my family. I got into trouble with the law, spent two nights in the Orangeburg County Jail, lost my drivers license, accidentally back into a vehicle and left the scene. And guess what? GOD has carried me and helped me through it all! Thank You Father! Thank You Jesus!

God helped me to see that all these things that had happened to me were not drug related, but that it was the work of Satan and his rulers of darkness, his spiritual wickedness and demons was trying to destroy me and terminate my life, wanting to stop God's work in me. Listen, no foe can withstand God's power and God's will for you and I, will be done! And not even Satan can stop or terminate Gods plan for our life!

Sure I suffered, but I did not suffered like Jesus suffered for me! Remember what happened to Jesus after He died. He rose to "LIFE" again! I died to my sinful nature and God has given me a new life. Yeah, I kept stumbling and falling and I was allowed to suffer because of my disobedience to God. I have surrendered my life to God and diligently begin to seek His kingdom and His righteousness and yes, all things are being added unto me. I am being abundantly blessed.

I always keep God first in all that I do. In fact, I don't do anything without consulting Him first. Because I know that I can do nothing, absolute nothing without Him. I don't want to do anything without God, not even think! This is why I pray each and every day that God make my thoughts agreeable to His will so that it is His plans that are established and succeed in this wonderful life that He has given to me!

I choose to live my life showing the love, mercy and grace that Our Father God has given to me! I choose to live my life to not only serve, but to please my Heaven Father! He is so worthy to be served and pleased! And I am determined to do just that for the rest of my days!

Audrey F. Evans-Ford

"IF"

If I had only!
If I had only listened!
If I had listened to my Dad I would have lead and been steadfast!
If I had only listened to my Mom I would have succeeded and not be needy!
If I had only listened to my Teacher I would have excelled instead of being expelled!
If I had only listened to my Preacher I would have been a teacher!
If I had only listened to Jesus I would not have used dope to cope!
If I had only listened to Jesus and resisted sin, I would not have needed to start life over again!
Thank you Jesus, for renewing my life. Thank you Jesus I am no longer an "If!"
"IF" an "Ignorant Fool!"

By Audrey F. Evans-Ford

A Plan

I am not trying to force my beliefs or ways on anyone. I know that I love God and I want to live according to His laws and principles. And yes, it is my hope and desire that I can in some small way or measure fulfill the will of God! It is Gods will that has made it possible for me to help my Brothers and Sisters to find their way back to Him. And for those who do not know Him, hopefully they will get to know and love Him! I am just God's child trying to do His will. Desiring to serve and please Him!

Desiring to be obedient to the word of Our Father God and live according to His principles. Through the empowerment of the Holy Spirit, I came up with a plan to help me to walk steady and consistently in the word. And I just want to share it with you.

One day I was just sitting and thinking about God and what could I do to please Him. I wanted to find a way that I could do His will and stop stumbling. So, I thought about it. We make plans everyday to do just about everything in our lives. From taking a bath, brushing our teeth, cleaning our house, going to work, grocery shopping, going to the Doctor, filling the car with gas etc... We have planned these things so well that they are not even planned anymore. They are just done, why? Because they have become routine to us now! They are a part of our everyday life.

Then it hit me! If we can make plans to do all these other things in life, then why can't we make plans for Jesus to be a part of our everyday lives?

If we made plans to make Jesus a part of our everyday lives, then our lives with Him will be a natural part of our every day lives! We would become closer to Him. And by becoming closer to Jesus we will naturally begin to live as Jesus would have us to live. I believe that this would make us less accessible to sin. For those who walk with Jesus, do not walk in sin. And they are careful in the things that they say and do. I am not just talking about going to Church on Sunday and Bible study midweek. I am talking about keeping Jesus in our lives everyday, every moment, with every thought.

Yes, we should make a plan to always include Jesus in our everyday lives. Let Jesus be your first thought of the day. Keep Him in our mind as He is in our heart. When we are making decisions, we should pray about them and ask Jesus for guidance. Let our conversations include Jesus and let His name be magnified and glorified. This is the plan that I have come up with for myself. It is as simple as ABC and 123!

A - cknowledge God!
B - elieve in God!
C - all on God!

1. Keep God first in my life, loving and honoring Him!
2. Remember Jesus is my best friend!
3. I Trust and Believe only in Christ with my life!

If you make these ABC's and 1,2,3's an everyday part of your life, I believe that not only will you fulfill the will and desires of God, but that you will please Him. In fact, I know you will. So, when trouble comes your way remember the ABC's and 123's.

I am no Saint, but I sure am doing all that I can to be one. I am determined to serve my Father God and to please Him. I want to be all that my Father has created and made me to be! And again I hope that I have helped you in some way to do the same.

It is written in the book of Isaiah 41:9-10 that our Father God said, "Thou who I have taken from the ends of the earth and called thee from the chief men thereof and said unto thee, **"Thou art my servant: I have chosen thee, and not cast thee away. Fear thou not: for I am with thee. Be not dismayed yea I will uphold thee with the right hand of my righteousness!"**

***NOTE: If you decide to follow this plan, and for some reason you slip away from it! Don't Worry! Because if you are diligently seeking the Lord and have a sincere and repenting heart, all you need to know is that Our God is watching you, protecting you and helping you!

Be assured, that where your plan may fail:
Gods Plan "WON'T" Fail!

The Bible

One day I had a conversation with my baby brother about the Bible. He had mentioned that he was going to start reading the Bible and he also commented on my knowledge of the Bible. We spoke of his knowledge of the Bible, which was little to none at that time. Well I immediately explained to him that it was okay, because the Holy Spirit will tell him what God wants him to know.

I had no idea that I would be sitting here today writing a story in reference to the "Bible" because of the conversation that my baby brother and I had. Since that conversation about the Bible, I have given a lot of thought to why many people do not read the Bible. I thought about the reasons that I did not read the Bible, they were:

1. I was living in sin.
2. I did not have time.
3. I thought that the Bible was complicated.
4. I could not pronounce the names.
5. It was to many thee's and thou's.

Yes, these were my reasons. I can honestly say that I believe that there are many people that do not read the Bible for at least one of these reasons. Well, the first reason is the main reason that I did not read the Bible, I was living in sin and I was not even thinking about what sin was and what sin was'nt. And surely I was not thinking about reading the Bible. Hey, I knew the 23rd Psalm and I knew "Now I lay me down to sleep and Our Father who art in Heaven." I did not learn these prayers from the Bible, my mother taught them to me when I was a child, so I was good to go. This is what I thought!

Since I have surrendered my life to Christ and have given up sin, I have time to read the Bible. I realized the Bible is not complicated. The names in the Bible are not really that hard to pronounce and I don't mind all the thee's and thou's! In all essence, I can speak the truth and say to you, there is absolutely nothing complicated about the Bible! Let me tell you why.

The Bible is no longer complicated for me because I surrendered my life to Christ and I am the righteousness of our Father! I no longer live in harmony with the world, nor with my flesh. And I am assured of this because it is written in Romans 8:9 that being made the righteousness of God, I live with His Spirit who dwells in me. And it is the Spirit Himself that bears witness with my human spirit that I am God's child and I am His heir and joint heir with Jesus! I have been set free from enslavement and corruption. I have glorious freedom in Jesus, because I am Gods child. And this is written in Roman 8:16-17 and 21says that I am Gods servant and He keeps fast hold of me. He watches over me because I am His righteous one. God Himself is my helper!

I realize that when I was in the world living in sin, I was not thinking about God or Jesus. In fact the only time I thought about God or Jesus was when something went wrong and I could not fix it myself, mainly a broken heart! Yeah, the broken heart will do it! The broken heart will send you to your knees weak, weary, crying, begging and pleading to God for His help! Oh, this I know and I am telling you so! I have been there and done that many times!

There were times in the past that I felt as though I did not know how to pray. Well, I decided that if I would read the Bible then I could learn how to pray. But, each time that I would begin to read the Bible it seemed to become more and more complicated for me to read and understand. So I would just say forget it and put it down. And to be totally honest with you, after the last time I put the Bible down it took me at least fifteen to twenty years before I picked it up again to read.

Today I realize that it was the work of Satan! Of course, who else? I was living in his world doing his thing, my thing, whatever and everything that he would tempt or suggest that I do. I was living in his kingdom were he rules! I was unconsciously aware at that time that I was trying to escape his kingdom. Satan was'nt, he was very much aware of what I was trying to do and he could not allow that! Satan could not allow me to read the Bible nor learn how to pray. Satan did not want me to know that God loves me and that it is to God whom I belong and not him! There was no way Satan was about to let me find out these things without a fight! It was Satan that blocked the word of God and made the Bible complicated for me to read and understand.

Acknowledge, Beware and Recognize

I Thank God that I belong to Him! I Thank my Father for helping me! God is your helper too! Guess what? It is written in the Bible in 1Corinthians 2:11-13 that **"No man learn the things of God except by the Spirit of God!"** The things we speak are not words taught by human wisdom but by the spirit of God. This means that when you surrender your life to God, you become righteous in Him through Jesus Christ. Being the righteousness of our Father we inherit all that belongs to Him. Yes, even His Spirit! And because the Spirit of God abides in us, the Spirit announces and declares the word of God to us!

The Bible confirms the word of God to us! I am assured of this. You see, the Holy Spirit announces and declares the word of God to me. Every time that I read the Bible, which is everyday now, I always read something that the Holy Spirit has already spoken to me. The Holy Spirit helps me to obtain knowledge and to understand the Bible, as well as confirm the word of God!

"The Bible and The Holy Spirit Confirms the Word of God!"

"Read And Enjoy The Bible!"

Audrey F. Evans-Ford

Sit or Stand!

Yeah! Just do it! Sit or Stand! It really does not matter which one you do, just as long as you do it. Trust in God no matter what!

How many times have you heard, said or have been told to "Stand on the word of God?" You have probably heard it, said it and been told this so many times that you cannot remember the count! I know I cannot remember how many times that I have heard it, how many times I have said it or how many times that I have been told to "Stand on the Word of God!"

And yet, even though the times are countless that I have heard it, said it and been told to just "Stand on Gods Word" I still at times fall and start doubting Gods word. I am not a gambling woman, but I assure you that you too at times will fall. And if you belong to God you have. You see, during the times that we are standing on the Word of God, we are sure, confident, full of joy and even at rest knowing that our Father always answers our prayers. THEN!

The Devil, our adversary sees our confidence and joy and he is saying, "Oh No! I can't stand it!" Hating to see us so confident and so full of joy, Satan does what he loves doing, he gets to work on stealing our joy and breaking our confidence in the word of God, causing us to doubt.

Satan says things such as; "I know you don't really think that God is going to answer your prayer this time. Child you have sinned one time to many!" Yeah, Satan wants to put fear in you now causing you to question God. Will God forgive me this time? Is this my seven times seventy time yet? Satan has you doubting now. Oh but it does not stop there. He continues to rub it in. Saying things to you like, "Do you really think that God is going to forgive you this time? Are you really sure? Are you positive that God will keep His word? Just what makes you think that He will? Maybe God does not want to give to you what you ask this time. Oh, you asked God to give to you the desire of your heart. How sweet! What makes you believe that He will do it? After all, you don't deserve it! Suppose it is not Gods desire to give to you your desire, not this time. Now what?

Do you know what just happened to you? Satan has just attacked your mind weakening you, causing you to doubt the word of God.

Acknowledge, Beware and Recognize

And the thing about what Satan has just done is nothing new. He uses the same techniques and weapons all the time. And most of the time and sometimes all of the time, we fall for it! Don't we feel dumb!

I get so angry with myself when I allow Satan to mess with my mind like that. I know that Satan is a liar! You would think that after so many attacks from Satan, with him using the same old weapons and techniques that I would be more aware of them and catch Satan's every fiery dart and quench them! No not me, I would fall every time! I confess, he still gets me at times, but not as often! Thank God! For example right now, today he is really trying very hard to mess with my mind. I am telling you, Satan never, ever gives up! But it is okay! I have learned to be obedient to the word of God! I have learned to be aware and watch out for the Devil!

Let me tell you, not only am I going to Stand on the word of God, but I am going to sit, lie down, sleep and even bathe in the word of God. Know why? Because it is the word of God that I even exist! It is written in the Holy Bible in John 1:1 that in the beginning was the word, the word was God and the word is God! That is all I need to know! Think about it, in the beginning there was nothing but darkness and God spoke (words) and said let there be light, and sure enough we have light! It is Gods spoken words that there is life. And nothing apart from God exist!

I lie to you not, even right now as I am writing this story Satan is attacking me big time. He does not want me to write this story, but guess what? It is He (the Holy Spirit) that lives in me that is greater than he (Satan) that is in this world. Thank you Jesus!

Listen, God does not care about what you have done. Only thing that matter to Him is what you are doing now. And if you surrender your life to Him and repent of your sins, not only will He forgive you, but He will also bless you. And yes, God will give to you the desires of your heart as well! Why? Because it is Gods desire to give to you, your desires so that your joy, gladness and delight be full, complete and overflowing! God wants you to be full of joy in every area of your life. God wants you to be prosperous, healthy and happy!

Here is some food for thought: Think about this, Satan was not always the Devil, he once was Gods favorite angel named Lucifer. Well as Lucifer, the Devil was not happy with all that God had given to him. He wanted more, he wanted Gods throne! I am talking to you about one who was not satisfied at all with Gods love and blessings.

He wanted our Fathers throne! Lucifer wage war in heaven and began to cause a ruckus and God was not even about to allow that to be, so God cast Lucifer down from heaven to the earth! Read about it the book of Isaiah 14:12-20.

Now really think about this, Lucifer wanted Gods throne and he waged war in heaven against God to get the throne. Okay God cast him out of heaven and down to earth. And guess what? Satan aka Lucifer has a kingdom. He is the ruler of this world.

So, if God has allowed Lucifer to have a kingdom to rule after he had turned on Him, why would you think that God would not give to you what you have asked for? I mean it is not as though we deliberately sin against Him. Do we? We love Him! Don't we? We are not trying to overthrow Him and take His throne. Are we? We have no desire to rule Gods kingdom. Do we? We just want to live in it with Him! Don't we? Think about it!

Look we all know that Satan does not want you and I to believe that God loves us just as much as He loved him, Lucifer. Satan does not want us to know that God always answer our prayers no matter what the situation is or the circumstances are, there is nothing impossible for God and there is nothing that God won't do for us if we ask Him! Why? Because He loves us!

It is written that Our Father God says ask anything, whatsoever of Him in the name of Jesus and it will be done. And Jesus tells us in the book of Matthew 7:7 to keep on asking and it will be given. Jesus says that everyone that asks receives! But, it is written in the book of James 1:6 that we must "keep asking in faith" not doubting at all. In 1 John 5:10 it is written that for us not to have faith in the word of God, is to call God and liar! This is blasphemy against God and a sin!

NOW, DO YOU SEE WHY SATAN WANTS YOU TO DOUBT GOD? When Satan causes you and I to doubt God, he also causes us to sin against our Father and he blocks and delays our blessings and our answered prayers!

In the book of Isaiah 55:11 it is written that Our Father God says that His word that goes forth from His mouth will not return void. It will prove to be. Our Father watches over His word! And, if this is not a good enough reason for you to have faith, then check this out: God magnifies His word above His name!

What other better reason could you possibly have to **Stand, Sit, Lay, Bathe** and **even Sleep on the word of God**?
"Stand on Gods Word or Fall in Satan Lies!"

Audrey F. Evans-Ford

The Summary

My greatest joy today is that I surrendered my life to Jesus. I thank Him and praise Him for redeeming me, giving me new life. Now that I have surrendered my life to Christ I can clearly see the sin in the world. There are so many people that are blind because of Satan lies and deceit. And sin has become a life style for many people. Unfortunately they do not even recognize it and they do not believe that God will bring down His wrath upon them!

These people today live their lives like those that lived in So'dom and Gomorrah, in sin and not even thinking about repenting! In the book of Genesis 18:20-32 tells of how Abraham pleaded with God for So'dom and Gomorrah asking Him not to bring them to ruin. Abraham approached Our Father God and asked Him would He really sweep away the righteous with the wicked? Abraham asked God that supposed he could find fifty righteous men in the city. Will He then pardon the city for the sake of fifty that are righteous?

Abraham pleaded with God saying that it is unthinkable of Him that He would act in such a manner to put to death the righteous man with the wicked! Abraham kept taking the number down until he got down to ten. So, God told Abraham that he would not bring the city to ruin on account of ten righteous men. Guess what? There were not even ten righteous men in the city. And God brought it to ruin!

The cities of So'dom and Gomorrah had Abraham to plead for them. But, Guess what? We have Jesus! Jesus lived, was beaten, tortured, hung, crucified with nails, died and rose from the dead, so that we would have everlasting life. As Christians believing and knowing that Jesus suffer and died for us, don't you think that we should not take His dying for us upon the cross for granted? I did and I am truly sorrow that I did. I thank Jesus for loving me unconditionally and forgiving me!

I don't believe that there is one Christian that deliberately takes Jesus dying on the cross for granted. I know that it is the work of Satan that causes Christians to sin. He is trying to steal, kill and destroy them! This is the purpose of his existence.

Acknowledge, Beware and Recognize

This book has been written to expose Satan, his lies and weapons. This book has been written to help those who do not know him to become aware of him, acknowledge him and recognize his works. In the Bible in 1 Peter 5:8 it is written that Jesus said for us to "Keep our senses and be watchful" for the adversary the Devil seeks to steal, kill and destroy."

Satan is going to continue to try to convince you to sin. And he is not going to tell you that, "Those of us who continue to present ourselves to anyone as a slave to obey him, that we are a slave of his. He is not going to tell you that there is death in view for you. This is written in the book of Roman 6:12. Satan is not going to tell you that if a man knows how to do what is right and yet does not do it, it is a sin! This is written in the book of James 4:17. And Satan is not going to tell you that if you continue to sin that when the appointed time comes, God will say to you "Be on your way from me, I do not know you!" and that you have been cursed into the everlasting fire prepared for the Devil and his angels. And this is written in the book of Matthew 25:41.

Listen, Stop! Letting Satan choke the word of God! He is always turning the word of God around to serve his purpose, which is to destroy you! Satan knows the Bible backwards and forwards. In other words, Satan knows the Bible better than you and I. Satan existed thousands of years before you and I came to be. Let me give you one example of how Satan will take the word of God and turn it around to serve his purpose and have you and I disobey God. Satan will convince you to sin, telling you that it is okay to sin because, [and he says this with such arrogance] your Father God will forgive you for all your sins! I am telling you, DON'T DO IT! Don't do it! Don't Sin! Satan is a liar! Remember what I just told you, "If a man knows how to do what is right and yet does not do it, it is a sin for him!

Look, what I am telling you is this; if you want a better life, then you need to, if you have not already done so, surrender your life to Christ Jesus and stop taking life for granted. I admit that at first it may seem boring, mundane and a total drag. But, guess what? It really is not. This is what Satan wants you to think. And believe me Satan is going to attack you every step of the way, he does not want you free from the bondage of sin.

If you stumble or even fall, guess what? It is okay because Jesus is right there with you to pick you up! He will help you and place your feet on solid ground for real! It is written in James 3:2 that "If anyone does not stumble in the word, this one is a perfect man, able to bridle also his own body." Jesus expects you to stumble because He knows that you are not perfect!

I am not asking you for my sake, but for your very own sake, withdraw from sin! If you are tired of suffering and being unhappy give Jesus a chance in your life. Try it His way! You can have joy and peace right now, right here on earth. You do not have to wait to go to heaven!

If you want to have joy, peace, prosperity, wholeness in your body and soundness of your mind, then it is imperative for you to remember that a man that knows how to do what is right and yet does not do it, it is a sin for him! Sinners are not blessed until they surrender and repent!

Look at all the things that are going on around you each and every day. Does it look like time is on you side? I think not!

According to the book of "Revelations" the judgment is very near. In fact it is nearer to us than most of us are willing to believe. And it is truly close enough for all of us to repent of our sins and become obedient to the word of God!

Look, Jesus Himself said that He does not know the day nor the hour that the end will come. Our Father kept the time of the end in His own jurisdiction. It is written in the book of Acts 1:7 that "It does not belong to you nor I to get knowledge of the times and seasons which the Father has placed in His own jurisdiction." So knowing that death and the end is in view and near, we should surrender our lives now to God.

Is the "Judgment" today? Is it tomorrow? When is it? Do you really want to take a chance on going to **"HELL?"** Satan wants you! Is this not enough for you to withdraw from sin? Our Father Gods loves you!

We all have been given a free will to choose our final place of everlasting life: **"HEAVEN or HELL"**. You need to choose soon! Like I said, as in yesterday!

I have had a taste of Hell; **"I CHOOSE HEAVEN!"**

D *rugs are a device used to*
R *uin us and destroy us, that is*
U *sed by Satan, to take us from*
G *od our Father and from our*
S *avior Jesus Christ!*

Audrey F. Evans-Ford

AFFORD

I AFFORD, can't! NO! I cannot afford the wages of "SIN." And even if I could, I wouldn't want to pay it. Why would I want to? The price is high. There is no refund. The price is final. The price is death!

God gave me life and I had to pay no price! God love me so much that He sent His only begotten Son into this world to live, suffer and die for me! Jesus paid the price for my life, by giving His "LIFE!"

This gift of life that my loving Father has given to me, I am determine to keep it and live it the way He would have me to live it! Doing His will, loving Him, praising Him, glorifying His name and always Thanking Him!

Audrey F. Evans-Ford

About the Author

Audrey has no PHD' s, MD' s or any other type of degree's. She considers herself to be just one of God's children that was once lost in a crazy mixed up world. She had no idea where she belonged or what her purpose in life was. But after many years of hurt, pain, heartbreak, drugs and praying, God delivered her. Audrey confesses that God healed her and filled her with His Spirit, delivering her from this present evil world and translated her into His kingdom.

Audrey takes no credit for the wisdom and knowledge in this book. She gives all the credit to God for His awesome work in her. She thanks God for calling her into union with Him and Christ Jesus and using her effectually in the body of Christ to serve Him. She confesses that every word that you will read or have read in this book is the work of God and His Holy Spirit that resides within her.

Printed in the United States
1123400002B